Losing

What is the WI?

If you have enjoyed this book, the chances are that you would enjoy belonging to the largest women's organisation in the country — the Women's Institutes.

We are friendly, go-ahead, like-minded women, who derive enormous satisfaction from all the movement has to offer. This list is long — you can make new friends, have fun and companionship, visit new places, develop new skills, take part in community services, fight local campaigns, become a WI market producer, and play an active role in an organisation which has a national voice.

The WI is the only women's organisation in the country which owns an adult education establishment. At Denman College, you can take a course in anything from car maintenance to paper sculpture, from book-binding to yoga, or word processing to martial arts.

All you need to do to join is write to us here at the National Federation of Women's Institutes, 39 Eccleston Street, London SW1W 9NT, or telephone 01–730 7212, and we will put you in touch with WIs in your immediate locality.

Losing Weight Naturally

Jane Fallon

CENTURY

LONDON · SYDNEY · AUCKLAND · JOHANNESBURG

First published in Great Britain in 1989 by
Century Hutchinson Ltd
Brookmount House, 62–65 Chandos Place,
Covent Garden, London WC2N 4NW

Century Hutchinson Australia (Pty) Ltd
89–91 Albion Street, Surry Hills,
New South Wales 2010, Australia

Century Hutchinson New Zealand Ltd
PO Box 40–086, 32–34 View Road, Glenfield,
Auckland 10, New Zealand

Century Hutchinson South Africa (Pty) Ltd
PO Box 337, Bergvlei 2012, South Africa

Set in Sabon by Input Typesetting Ltd, London
Printed and bound in Great Britain by
Mackays of Chatham Ltd, Chatham, Kent

British Library Cataloguing in Publication Data

Fallon, Jane
  Losing weight naturally.
  1. Physical fitness. Slimming. Diet
  I. Title II. Series 613.2'5

  ISBN 0–7126–2951–3

CONTENTS

IMPORTANT NOTE

The calories recommended for women do not, at any point in this book, apply to pregnant or nursing mothers. Women who are pregnant or nursing should not consider a weight-reduction diet until the baby is born and they are no longer nursing. A reduction in protein intake is emphatically not recommended for these women as the health of the child relies on both a higher-protein and higher-calorie intake during this time.

In addition, the calorie recommendations included here do not apply to anyone under the age of 21 years. The diet programmes described in this book are based on dietary recommendations made to the general population to reduce fat intake and increase fibre intake. If you wish to begin a diet programme, it is always wise to meet with your doctor to confirm that there are no medical reasons why you should not undertake a change of diet. Any dietary change should be agreed between you and your doctor. Diagnosis and treatment of medical conditions is a responsibility shared between you and your doctor, and neither the author nor publisher of this book can accept responsibility for the consequences of dietary treatment based on the recommendations described herein.

CHAPTER ONE

What Have You Got To Lose?

You're standing in the High Street and suddenly you hear cries from an upstairs window nearby. Thick black smoke is pouring out of it, and a woman and child are screaming for help.

A siren sounds in the distance and a fire engine appears with its ladders and hoses. However, when the doors open, instead of strong, slim-waisted firemen striding to the rescue, a group of breathless, roly-poly men lumber slowly forward and discuss who among them is fit enough to climb the ladder and save the mother and child.

A bad dream? No. It's all roo real. For in 1986, a three-year study was completed and a report* drawn up on the physical preparedness and stamina of the staff of the British fire service. The results were horrifying: half of the 40,000 firemen working in the country were considered to be overweight, and approximately 6,500 of these men were so obese as to be unable to perform their normal duties – such as climbing that ladder! – without themselves suffering from considerable physical stress.

You see, even physically active people – such as firemen – can all too easily fade into flab. When we look at the rest of the British population, the picture is equally podgy. In 1984 the Department of Health and Social Security published figures showing that approximately nine million women and nearly eleven million men were 'very overweight'. In other words, 32% of British women and 39% of British men weigh more, much more, than they ought to.

Of course, Britain isn't alone in being submerged under excess blubber. Many developed countries share our predicament. Thirty-four million Americans are officially classified as 'obese' – that's one out of every five adults in the country. But perhaps

* Commissioned by the Home Office, conducted by a team from the former physiology department at Chelsea College, University of London, from 1981 to 1984.

the most disturbing part of the picture is the situation that children find themselves in. In some areas of Britain, nearly 80% of children are destined to be the obese adults of the future. By the time we're ten years old, our diet and lifestyle is often well established and difficult or impossible to change. If we've been taught bad eating habits, then we'll probably go on eating badly all our lives.

Why should children be particularly at risk? Well, there are a number of reasons. In the years following the war, well fed babies and children were just one of the welcome signs of peace and growing prosperity. Bulging bellies were a positive delight after the shortages and hardships of the war years. Parents took pride and pleasure in showing off their bouncing babies, as a sign of growing affluence.

Another body-blow to healthy eating came when school meal nutrition standards were abolished in 1980, in the first round of public spending cuts. Children are now allowed to select and purchase their own school lunches on a cafeteria-style system. Many children buy food at local cafés instead. Even the Department of Health's own survey of the effects of abolishing standards has shown that four out of five children are eating an 'unhealthy' diet, including too much saturated fat and too few essential nutrients. They eat more chips, crisps, and other potato products than any other single food, and three times more chips, cakes and biscuits than the average household.

Also to blame for the rise in youthful body fat is the fact that today's children are underactive when compared with the children of earlier generations. Their sedentary lifestyle (comprised of up to 20 hours spent watching television per week and greatly reduced numbers of hours spent in sports and games) predicts a sedentary lifestyle in adulthood, predisposing them to a wide range of physical and social problems.

Many voices have been raised in protest against the unhealthy diet that our children are eating, but little positive action seems to emerge. The 95,000-strong Assistant Masters and Mistresses Association produced a report which heavily criticized nutritional standards. 'There is now ample evidence that our national eating habits are unhealthy,' it said, 'and it could be that education authorities, however accidentally, are reinforcing bad eating habits which children should be educated out of, not encouraged to carry over into the home.'

'So worried were my staff', wrote one teacher, 'about the dietary implications of what has happened to the meals service that they wrote, unanimously, to the chairman of the education committee. Our letter was dismissed as being 'emotive' and 'sweeping' and we were told that there was no direct evidence of a link between ill health and a high intake of fried food.'*

But if our schools are producing a new generation of fatties, then the blame has to be shared with those parents who often say 'We'll let our children decide what they want to eat for themselves, when they are older', thinking, perhaps, that any standards they present to their children are, in some way, impositions, and mean deprivation. But if they *really* cared about the future happiness of the children, they would realise that people who are overweight are much more likely to suffer from cancer, heart disease and hypertension. They would also know that obese people are more prone to depression, lack of confidence, guilt and frustration, and are often victims of a social prejudice that labels them as 'unattractive', 'greedy' or 'weak-willed'. Studies have shown that the mortality rate rises rapidly for people weighing just 20% above normal – and the most common causes of death for overweight people are stroke, heart disease, high blood pressure and diabetes. Also, overweight women have a very elevated risk of contracting cancer of the lining of the uterus. After menopause, their breast cancer risk is higher, too.

Right now, it may seem impossible to you that you will ever become thin again. Well, let's be honest and admit that we still have an enormous amount to learn about obesity. No-one – other than an out-and-out charlatan – can *promise* to make you slim, trim and desirable. You may be overweight because of genetic or hormonal reasons, in which case dieting may not prove effective. But many people – probably *most overweight people* – are fat through other causes – perhaps social reasons, psychological ones, or through environmental factors. For example, if you now have 'middle-age spread', but previously used to be a normal weight, then you have an outstanding chance of regaining your former size. Although experts disagree over many issues relating to obesity, there is a clear consensus that a huge

* The *Guardian*, July 24, 1984.

number of people are overweight simply because they consume too much food. And *that* can be corrected – most definitely.

So before we begin, I want you to agree to abide by three simple rules I propose setting. Don't cheat. Don't be tempted to say to yourself, 'Well, maybe I'll give it a try, but if it gets too difficult, I can always stop.' That is a recipe for failure. Read the rules and then, if you can wholeheartedly and determinedly agree to abide by them, we can start to make some real progress . . .

RULE ONE:
Please – Give Your Guilt A Holiday

I wonder whether you've ever had any thoughts such as
- 'I'm fat because I'm a *bad* person, so I deserve to be overweight and unattractive.'
- 'I feel guilty about being overweight, so I console myself by eating.'
- 'No-one finds me attractive, so I might as well indulge myself with food, because eating is the only thing that gives me satisfaction.'

All these feelings are provoked by, and in turn cause, guilt. It is a vicious circle, one that traps you into a never-ending cycle of depression and compensation-eating. Guilt is not a *motivational* emotion. It usually *stops* us doing things, it gets in the way. We feel guilty when we *haven't* done something, in fact, it's just a way of coping with failure. In no way does it encourage and reward *positive* behaviour – which is what we're going to do.

It is inevitable, of course, that after a lifetime's training intended to make you feel guilty, you will at some point feel bad about a little backsliding. When this happens, you must say to yourself: 'I slipped a bit today. I feel bad about it, but there's nothing I can do now. Yesterday, I won the battle. Tomorrow, I'm going to win again. I refuse to surrender to guilty feelings, because they pull me backwards and downwards. I am more determined than ever before to suceed.'

Agreed? Good. Now for

RULE TWO:
Be Resolutely Steadfast With Other People

Have you ever encouraged other people to eat (or over-eat) with you, because it gave you an *excuse* to over-indulge yourself as well? If you have, you may well be about to have the tables turned on you. People who are not on diets often tempt, cajole and taunt dieters to over-eat. It makes them feel better, because they know that really, they should shed some pounds as well. It's good 'sport'. It provokes a bit of verbal sparring. Oh yes, people can be very thoughtless and cruel to dieters. Here's how to cope with it.

On the first occasion, simply say, 'Thanks for the offer, but I'm on a diet. I'm making good progress and I don't want to spoil it all now. I'm sure you understand.'

End of discussion. Start talking about something more interesting. At this stage, you will find out who your real friends are. A real friend will realise that you're serious and won't press food on you. Others, however, may not be so kind. They will somehow take additional pleasure in tempting you even after you have explained yourself. For these bothersome, insensitive people we have a real knock-out punch in store. When you agree to rule two, immediately prepare a small note (do it now!) and copy it several times. Be sure to carry two or three of these around in your wallet or bag all the time, ready for just such an occasion. This is how it reads:

'The diet I'm adhering to won't allow me to do what you're suggesting. It's tough sticking to a diet, but I'm determined to see it through. As a friend, please help me to succeed by not placing obstacles in my way — I'll value you all the more for it.'

Silently, give them the note. Watch them study it. See the new look of respect on their faces. It will work, because its message is powerful, direct and so unexpected.

RULE THREE:
Recognize — But Don't Pamper — The Child Inside

There is a little urge inside you, as there is inside all people who habitually over-eat, that behaves just like a small child. It wants satisfaction. It doesn't want to be reasoned with. It wants everything now. It doesn't want to wait. It wants to be pampered and spoilt.

First of all, you must recognize and understand this child-like urge. For virtually the whole of human history, food has been *scarce*. Only in the past 100 or 200 years has it been possible to rely on constant, year-round availability of food. Our bodies – and our inner drives – have not yet adapted to this recent overabundance of food. So whenever we see food – on the table, in advertisements, in shops, or wherever – our first and most powerful instinct is summed up in three letters: EAT!

When food supplies have been uncertain – as they have been for most of recorded time – it makes sense to eat whenever you have the opportunity, because it could be a long, long time until you get to eat again. This survival strategy has worked extremely well – until now.

As recently as a few hundred years ago, your instinct to eat whenever you could would have been a blessing – which could well have seen you through tough times, which others might not have survived. Now, however, we in the West are no longer threatened by the prospect of famine. We have more than enough food for everyone. But that same urge to eat which would have kept you alive a few hundred years ago is now – ironically – proving to be a life-threatening liability.

There is another instinct, too, which for thousands of years has proved to be a great advantage to our species, but which is now turning out to be a hazard. We humans also show a great deal of interest in 'new' food. In evolutionary terms, the species that is ready and willing to adapt its diet as circumstances change will have the upper hand over a species which doesn't adapt. But here's the big problem. Today, almost *every* food you see advertised on television is promoted as being 'new'. Have you ever wondered why?

The answer is that it exploits a natural instinct deep within our species which prompts us to experiment with all types of new food. It's worked very well for us in the past, but now, with so many new brands and types of food around, it's a recipe for tragedy.

Yet another instinct that has been turned upside down over the past 100 or 200 years involves the use of advertising images showing food being eaten by socially attractive people. Like rats

6

and many other omnivores, we prefer to be social eaters. If food is being eaten by a crowd of people we like or identify with, then (so our instincts tell us) that food is likely to be safe and edible. Again, this instinct is widely exploited by the people who sell food to us. Just look at the advertisements, and you'll begin to see the manipulation at work.

By now, you should realize that your urge to eat is instinctive. You should also realize that it is an instinct that many food manufacturers can profitably exploit for their own interests.

This is why I suggest you treat your urge to eat in the same way as you'd treat a small child. Hear the voice, but don't surrender to the pressure. Instead, try to understand it. Recognize that it is a voice from the past, whose main concern was to protect you and ensure your survival in dramatically different times to these. Don't let that child dominate your food behaviour, because the risks of doing so – as we've seen – are infinitely more serious for you personally.

CHAPTER TWO

Watching Your Figure

A lot of dieting seems to be carried out with a pencil and calculator: that is because most diets encourage you to count those mysterious things called 'calories', and to do that, it seems as if you sometimes need to be a mathematical wizard. You'll be pleased to learn that this book doesn't emphasize iron-handed calorie-counting. Losing weight is all about feeling fitter again, not about going on a protracted hunger-strike. First of all, then, let's consider what calories are, and why dieters worship them . . .

BURN, BABY, BURN!

Do you remember when your mother used to tell you, in exasperated tones, to 'go outside and burn off your extra energy' when you seemed too energetic to fit in the house? When she said 'burn' she was absolutely right, because food is converted into energy by a process of oxidation, sometimes called combustion or 'burning'. Food supplies you with the energy you need to grow, move, think, speak, dance, laugh and all the hundreds of activities that fill your life.

The food you eat is broken down through a series of mechanical and chemical actions in your digestive system to supply you with the basic materials necessary for health. The vitamins and minerals in your food are made available to keep your various systems regulated, the proteins are used for tissue growth and repair and the fats and carbohydrates are converted, through oxidation, into energy and heat. Foods are rarely made up of *only* protein or *only* vitamins and minerals, however – they usually include fat and carbohydrates as well. The quantity of fat and carbohydrate will vary, of course, from food to food, making it difficult to know precisely how much of these energy-producing substances you are consuming. Therefore a system of measuring the energy value of food has been established which converts all food into its potential for supplying heat. The unit of measurement is called a 'calorie', and, one calorie supplies enough heat to raise the temperature of 1 litre of water from 15°C to 16°C.

Sometimes, perhaps on food labels or packaging, you will see calories abbreviated to 'Kcal'. This is short for 'kilocalorie', and is the more precise, and scientific, way to express calories. A kilocalorie is 1000 calories, so when you say you need 2000 calories a day, you actually mean 2000 Kcal. Don't be confused by all this, because in nutritional language, everyone says 'calories' when they really mean 'kilocalories'.

The really important thing to remember is that your body is converting the food you eat into energy. Three elements of your diet do *not* supply energy: water, vitamins and minerals are all health-giving and entirely calorie free. In other words, they don't supply you with energy, but they do supply you with nutrients and fluid that is essential to good health. The remaining three elements of your diet are protein, fat and carbohydrate, and each of these *does* convert into energy.

Carbohydrates
These are the most important energy producers available to us, and they are present in three forms: simple (sugars), complex (starches), and cellulose (fibre). Simple and complex carbohydrates supply energy at a rate of approximately 4 calories per gram. Cellulose, or fibre, does not supply energy but aids in the digestion of food and the assimilation of vitamins and minerals. Simple carbohydrates are included in table sugar, fruits, honey and other highly refined or obviously sweet foods. They are converted very rapidly into glucose or 'blood sugar' which supplies instant energy to your brain, muscles and nerves. Complex carbohydrates are also converted into glucose or 'blood sugar' but they are converted slowly, over a much longer period of time. They are considered more beneficial than simple carbohydrates for your long-term health because they produce a steady trickle of glucose which prevents great fluctuations in the level of sugar in the blood. Such fluctuations can be stressful to the body, and in some people may contribute to the onset of diabetes.

Complex carbohydrates are contained in foods such as fruits, vegetables, nuts, seeds, grains, legumes and pulses. When consumed in a fairly unprocessed, or whole, condition these foods also provide fibre, or cellulose. An excess of either simple or complex carbohydrates will be stored in your body as fat.

Protein
This is second only to water as the most plentiful substance in your body. Much of your body tissue is made up of protein, and these tissues are constantly being repaired and replaced by the protein your body makes and by that which you take in your diet. Protein is comprised of a collection of amino acids which are bound together in various forms. As protein foods are digested, the proteins break apart into their amino acids and get to work repairing and building tissue and regulating the formation of hormones, blood, enzymes and antibodies.

Protein supplies about 4 calories per gram, the same as carbohydrate. However, it is not a good idea to think of protein as an energy source. Your body will always attempt to derive its energy needs from carbohydrates which are easier for it to break down. If it doesn't get enough energy from the carbohydrate part of your diet, it will begin to convert fat – either in your food or in your body. Only if, for some reason, it is unable to convert sufficient carbohydrate and fat into energy, will your body set to work converting protein into energy. However, it does not convert the protein in your diet, it converts the protein in your body which is your muscle tissue! This is to be avoided at all costs. Loss of muscle tissue will undermine your health and make it more difficult for you to lose body fat.

The majority of diets in this book will not recommend a high-protein intake because any surplus dietary protein is converted into fat in your body. If you continue to eat a high-protein diet (or a high-calorie diet) a cycle of excess is established in which your body fat increases beyond what is healthy and your body is stressed through the conversions it has been forced to make. Complex disease patterns can result, including diabetes, liver problems, kidney disorders and cardiovascular diseases.

Fat
This is a crucial part of your make up, no matter how awful you think it is at present. If you are a woman you need appro-

ximately 22% of your body weight as fat, if you are a man something closer to 15%. For most people, it is easy to acquire this amount of body fat and persons who are very active, such as elite athletes, are usually the only exceptions – they may have to work hard to keep their percentage of body fat up to 10 or 12%.

Fat is the most concentrated form of energy in your diet. Each gram of fat you consume is worth 9 calories, as compared to 4 calories for the same amount of protein or carbohydrate. As well as being concentrated, however, fat is also an efficient storehouse of energy. Any surplus of carbohydrate, protein or fat in your food is converted by your body into tidy, high-calorie parcels of fat. These conversions do not work in reverse, however. Fat does not convert into either protein or carbo-hydrate. Once you have stored a surplus of fat, the only way of reducing that surplus is to convert the fat into energy. After all, that is why your body stored it away in the first place!

FAT STORAGE AND STARVATION

Carbohydrates, proteins and fats may all be converted into energy in your body. However, your body needs a limited amount of energy to survive and perform all the activities you engage in. So any surplus of energy you allow in your diet – whether from protein, carbohydrate or fat – is stored in your body as fat. Remember, fat is the only food substance that is designed to be an energy storage unit. The others, carbohydrates and proteins, are designed, respectively, to supply fibre and your immediate energy needs, and your tissue repair and building needs. If you are too fat, your body is acting as a huge bank vault of stored energy. Now the question is, how can you use that stored energy and reduce your body fat?

Let me first discuss what *not* to do and, to illustrate my point, I'll tell you about a study of pregnant women in Keneba, Gambia.* In this village, women work extremely hard per-forming most of the strenuous agricultural work as well as carrying the water and firewood. Along with the other members of their village, they are almost continuously undernourished.

* *New Scientist*, 14 April, 1988.

To compound this shortage, the rainy season each year coincides with the gradual depletion of the previous year's harvest. So there is a temporary, predictable food shortage which further reduces the number of calories these people consume.

Yet, year after year, the young women of this village become pregnant and give birth, and all the while carry on working in the fields. How do these women manage to survive? The answer appears to be startlingly simple and effective. Their bodies respond to near-starvation by slowing their metabolic rate and, in the absence of adequate food, by utilizing their stores of body fat. So instead of using 1200 calories per day for subsistence, considered a minumum in affluent countries, these women use far fewer. And instead of consuming the extra calories they need, as happens in well-fed people, these women are, effectively, *consumed by* their extra calorie needs. They lose a significant amount of weight during this yearly food shortage because they are using up their own stores of body fat. Of course, once the food shortage is passed, they eat more and their bodies make certain that, once again, as much of this energy as possible is stored as fat.

Now consider a fat person in the West, who has probably never gone hungry in her life. This woman decides to go on a drastic, very low-calorie diet to reduce her body fat. After a few days of this self-imposed starvation, she will feel listless and possibly depressed. She will have a headache, a bad taste in her mouth and a profound regret that she ever thought of dieting. What has gone wrong?

The body of this dieter is receiving the same message as the body of that undernourished pregnant woman in Gambia. The message is 'slow right down. There is no food so it is necessary to conserve all the energy available.' Clever body! But what works for that Gambian woman – in fact, what keeps her alive – will keep the Western woman fat. Because once she stops the self-imposed starvation regime, her metabolic rate will not necessarily increase. Just like the Gambian woman, if hunger has become a chronic state, in one form or another, then the dieter may find that even a moderately low-calorie diet causes her to store fat!

None of the diets included in this book will require you to starve. Some 'cleansing' diets are included, but they are very short term, do not leave you feeling hungry and their correct use is explained in detail. It really makes no sense to trick your body into thinking it is starving. Instead, choose your foods with your health in mind and in sufficient quantities to meet your own personal calorie requirements.

WE CAN WORK IT OUT!

From the moment you were born, you required a certain amount of energy just to stay alive. You probably slept for 16 to 20 hours per day in your first few weeks of life but, even so, you needed energy to keep your heart beating, your brain active and your body temperature just right. The same was true as you passed through childhood into adolescence, and the same is true now that you are an adult. You still need a basic minimum of energy, supplied on a regular basis, just to stay alive.

The amount of energy you need for your very basic subsistence (i.e. enough to just tick over) is called your 'basal metabolism'. However, the precise amount of energy you need depends on your age, gender, size and also your general state of health. Look at these examples of two 'standard' people.

A 25-year-old woman weighing 112 pounds (8 stone) requires about 13 calories per pound of body weight every day. To find the number of calories she needs to supply her with her basal metabolic requirement, multiply 112 (pounds) by 13 (calories) to arrive at 1456 calories a day.

However, a 25-year-old man weighing 140 pounds (10 stone) requires about 14 calories per pound of body weight every day. Multiply 140 (pounds) by 14 (calories) to arrive at 1960, the approximate required number of calories to supply his basal metabolic needs.

As both of these sample people grow older, their basal metabolic needs will change. There are several reasons for this. First, as the years roll on, it is usual to lose a certain amount of lean body mass, or muscle tissue, and since it is muscle tissue that utilizes calories, a loss of muscle tissue means a lowered basal metabolism. For most of us, ageing means a reduction in the amount of physical activity we enjoy, which increases the likelihood of losing muscle mass. And it is often the case that age brings disease or disorders that force inactivity and/or loss of muscle mass upon us as well as affecting the efficiency with which the body metabolises.

Here's another quick rule of thumb to determine the number of calories you need to maintain your basal metabolism. If you are a woman, you may calculate that you need approximately 1 calorie per minute for your basic life functions like this: 1 calorie every minute, *multiplied by* 60 minutes in every hour, *multiplied by* 24 hours in the day, *equals* 1440 calories needed for your basal metabolism. For men, approximately 1.3 calories should be allowed per minute for basic life functions (this comes to 1872 calories per day). For older people, these requirements may be reduced to 0.9 calorie per minute for women and 1.1 calories per minute for men.

ENERGY FOR LIVING

So far, we've discussed 'basal metabolism' – the amount of energy you need just to keep your basic life functions going. However, any sort of activity beyond resting requires that you consume calories in addition to those needed for your basal metabolism. The nature of your activities, the length of time which you engage in them, and the regularity with which they are performed together influence the total number of calories you need in a day.

Here is a listing of activities, with their approximate calories per minute requirement, divided into the standard 'sedentary', 'light', 'moderate' and 'strenuous' levels.

Sedentary	Calories used per minute
Cooking	1.8
Sitting	1.4
Sleeping	1
Standing	1.7
Washing and ironing	3.5
Walking (slowly)	2.5
Dressing	3.5

Light

Assembly-line work	3.5
Bowls (recreation)	3.5
Carpentry	3.5
Domestic cleaning	3
Gardening (weeding, planting)	3.5
Golf	3.5
Sailing	4.4
Walking (normal pace)	3.5

Moderate

Cycling (level, unburdened)	4.5
Dancing	5.5
Gardening (hoeing, raking)	4.5
Swimming (slow, gentle)	6.5
Tennis	6.5
Walking (rapid)	6.5

Strenuous

Cycling (uphill, with load)	7
Football	7.5
Gardening (digging)	6
Lifting and carrying	7
Squash	8
Swimming (crawl, butterfly)	8.5
Walking (uphill, with load)	7.5

You should be able to judge, from this list, which category of activity you most often engage in. Then, using the figures given here and those for your basal metabolic needs, you can calculate your approximate calorie requirements for a 'normal' day.

Your basal metabolic needs may vary slightly over the years, but your daily calorie requirements will probably change from day to day and from month to month, depending on how you are spending your time. When your calorie requirements exceed the number of calories you take in, you are likely to start losing weight as your body uses its fuel reserves laid down as fat. On the other hand, if your calorie intake exceeds your calorie requirements you are likely to gain weight, as your body stores up fuel in the form of fat deposits.

YOUR PERSONAL CALORIE REQUIREMENTS

Using the chart which follows you may approximate your basal metabolic needs, your working calorie needs and your leisure-activity calorie requirements.* You should account for *all* the hours in your average day.

1) Your basal metabolic requirements:

Women	calculated at 1 calorie per minute
aged 20–39	1440
aged 40–59	1368–1300
aged 60–69	1170
aged 70+	1053

Men	calculated at 1.3 calories per minute
aged 20–39	1872
aged 40–59	1778–1689
aged 60–69	1520
aged 70+	1368

Your basal metabolic requirement: _____
divided by 24 hours: _____
multiplied by number of hours asleep: _____
equals your sleeping calorie requirement: _____ √

2) Now write down the amount of time you spend working, and the type of work that you do. Use the chart above to find out how many calories per minute each activity expends, and multiply this by the number of minutes spent on each activity to arrive at your total calorie expenditure at each type of work.

---

* The Food and Agriculture Organization of the United Nations (FAO) and The World Health Organization (WHO) 1974 report on the Expert Committee on Energy and Protein Requirements have recommended that basal calorie needs may be assumed to stay unchanged during a person's twenties and thirties, but that they drop in the decades which follow. Accordingly, the figures in this chart are approximated to comply with the reductions in basal metabolic needs that this committee has suggested.

Working activity	Calories per minute	× No. of minutes	= Calories
_____ @	_____	× _____	= _____
_____ @	_____	× _____	= _____
_____ @	_____	× _____	= _____
_____ @	_____	× _____	= _____
_____ @	_____	× _____	= _____
_____ @	_____	× _____	= _____

Total numbers of calories spent during
working activities   =_____√

3) Finally, do the same process for the remaining hours in the day.

Leisure activity	Calories per minute	× No. of minutes	= Calories
_____ @	_____	× _____	= _____
_____ @	_____	× _____	= _____
_____ @	_____	× _____	= _____
_____ @	_____	× _____	= _____
_____ @	_____	× _____	= _____
_____ @	_____	× _____	= _____

Total numbers of calories spent during
leisure activities   =_____√

Now simply add the three sub-totals together (those with a double-underline and marked with a √) to give your total calorie requirement for an average day.

1) Sleeping calorie requirements: _____
   plus
2) Working calorie requirements: _____
   plus
3) Leisure calorie requirements: _____
   equals
   Your total calorie requirement: _____

YOUR CORRECT WEIGHT

There are many factors to consider when attempting to ascertain your correct weight. Although there are many formulae for determining your weight and calorie status, in fact, the final decision about what is correct has to be yours. This is because what is correct for you might differ greatly from what is correct for another person with similar obvious characteristics. However, to give you guidelines within which to judge for yourself, here is a chart of recommended weights according to your gender, height and frame size.

Desirable Weights for Men and Women Aged 25 and Over*
MEN: wearing indoor clothing and shoes with 2.5cm (1 inch) heels.

Height	Small Frame in lbs	Medium Frame in lbs	Large Frame in lbs
5' 2"	112 – 120	118 – 129	126 – 141
5' 3"	115 – 123	121 – 133	129 – 144
5' 4"	118 – 126	124 – 136	132 – 148
5' 5"	121 – 129	127 – 139	135 – 152
5' 6"	124 – 133	130 – 143	138 – 156
5' 7"	128 – 137	134 – 147	142 – 161

* Prepared from data published by the Metropolitan Life Insurance Company, New York, 1959 and 1983.

MEN:(*continued*)

Height	Small Frame in lbs	Medium Frame in lbs	Large Frame in lbs
5' 8"	132 – 141	138 – 152	147 – 166
5' 9"	136 – 145	142 – 156	151 – 170
5' 10"	140 – 150	146 – 160	155 – 174
5' 11"	144 – 154	150 – 165	159 – 179
6' 0"	148 – 158	154 – 170	164 – 184
6' 1"	152 – 162	158 – 175	168 – 189
6' 2"	156 – 167	162 – 180	173 – 194
6' 3"	160 – 171	167 – 185	178 – 199
6' 4"	164 – 175	172 – 190	182 – 204

WOMEN: wearing indoor clothing and shoes with 5cm (2-inch) heels.

Height	in lbs	in lbs	in lbs
4' 10"	92 – 98	96 – 107	104 – 119
4' 11"	94 – 101	98 – 110	106 – 122
5' 0"	96 – 104	101 – 113	109 – 125
5' 1"	99 – 107	104 – 116	112 – 128
5' 2"	102 – 110	107 – 119	115 – 131
5' 3"	105 – 113	110 – 122	118 – 134
5' 4"	108 – 116	113 – 116	121 – 138
5' 5"	111 – 119	116 – 130	125 – 142
5' 6"	114 – 123	120 – 135	129 – 146
5' 7"	118 – 127	124 – 139	133 – 150
5' 8"	122 – 131	128 – 143	137 – 154
5' 9"	126 – 135	132 – 147	141 – 158
5' 10"	130 – 140	136 – 151	145 – 163
5' 11"	134 – 144	140 – 155	149 – 168
6' 0"	138 – 148	144 – 159	153 – 173

NOTE: for each year under 25, women between the ages of 18 and 24 should subtract 1 pound from the upper limit of their 'category'.

Weight measured without clothes may be 2 to 5 pounds less than that measured in indoor clothing.

Using this chart and your calculations regarding your daily calorie requirements, you may begin to form a picture of how much weight you need to lose, if any.

ARE YOU OVERWEIGHT?

Weigh yourself on a trustworthy set of scales, then compare your weight to the recommendations listed in the chart above. You will be able to tell at a glance whether you are well within, on the edges of, or exceeding the optimum weights listed for your height, frame size and gender. It is true that charts such as this are necessarily approximate. After using the chart, if you are still doubtful whether or not you are overweight, try pinching the underside of your upper arm. If the thickness of pinch is slightly under 2.5cm (1 inch) for a woman, slightly over 2.5cm (1 inch) for a man, then you may consider that you are not over fat.

Even if you are 'only' 5 pounds or so overweight, some health professionals feel strongly that you are eroding your health and should lose that 5 surplus pounds. However, the only accurate way of determining whether you really need to lose weight is to find out just how much of your body weight is fat and how much is muscle and bone – this is called your Lean Body Mass.

The percentage of body weight that is made up of fat is not an easy thing to measure. However, in a research laboratory or during a 'physical' (the total health assessment sometimes required by employers), you may be tested to determine what percentage of fat makes up your body weight. This test may be performed using a set of callipers placed to pinch the skin under your upper arm. The thickness of the pinch determines, approximately, the amount of fat you carry (as mentioned above, you can try this yourself).

In general, it is considered healthy for a woman to carry 22% of her body weight, and a man to carry 15% of his body weight, as fat. In the absence of accurate tests, however, how are you to know whether or not you are exceeding these limits?

I can offer three means of judging this. First, that you do a calculation of your daily calorie needs and then keep a record of your actual calorie intake every day for one week. You will need an ordinary calorie counter for this and a certain amount of determination to keep the record. Now simply do your sums! If your intake exceeds your requirements, then you can be fairly sure that you have accumulated extra fat.

Another quick way of estimating your degree of obesity is to find out how much your weight exceeds that recommended for your height, gender and frame size in the tables above – generally, a 5% excess implies that you are moderately overweight. Up to a 10% excess means that you are overweight. Between 10 and 15% excess and one is very overweight. Over 20% excess weight above the ideal and one is considered obese.

The third method of determining whether or not you are overweight is to look at yourself! You are the person who really knows whether or not you need to reduce the fat content of your body.

By now, you should have a good idea of your daily calorie requirements, and you should know to what extent you are overweight. You will find that the diets in the following chapters are not extremely punishing or restrictive, because one of the main aims of successful dieting is to re-train your appetite. Together, we want to encourage your mind and stomach to eat fewer, more healthy, calories. This is easier than it might seem at first glance. And although many dieters are tempted to resort to much more extreme measures, as we'll see in the next chapter, these are rarely successful, and may be more dangerous than you might suppose . . .

CHAPTER THREE

Why You Should Lose Weight Naturally

From this point onwards I will assume that you are fully committed to losing that surplus baggage you've been carrying around for too long now.

Before we consider different methods of losing weight, let's pause to think about the main causes of failure. You may have heard that 95% of dieters eventually regain the weight they lost through dieting. This is indeed depressing news, but rather than giving up before we've even started, we should ask ourselves *why* they fail.

The prime reason that diets fail is actually quite simple. In the majority of cases, it is because the dieter *did not commit themselves to a change of life*. Instead, they sought 'instant' results and 'gluttony without girth' diet programmes that could not possibly be adopted on an ongoing basis. The result of these attempts – and many people spend *years* of their lives going from one fad diet to the next – is usually a reaffirmation of what most obese people already feel: that they are lazy, ugly and failures. As well as losing their battle with obesity, people who fail to make these diets work for them over the long term lose self-confidence. And further, they are affronted on all levels: physically by the unhealthiness of the diet regime; mentally by the *angst* involved in dieting; and emotionally by the reiteration of failure.

It seems to me that the whole point of dieting is to *feel better* all round: better health prospects, better appearance, better feelings about yourself. Yet how often does dieting really achieve this, and if it does, how long for?

One of the basic problems inherent in most weight-reduction programmes is the fact that two overweight individuals can react very differently to the same diet. For instance, why is it possible for two overweight people, of the same size and weight, to go on identical diets and yet lose different amounts of weight?

Why do dieters lose weight at different speeds – some losing a rewarding amount in the first weeks, others having to wait two or three months for a significant loss? And how is it that two children, born into the same family and raised on the same dietary patterns, can grow up one thin, the other obese? The answers to these and many other questions evade us, even though year after year new studies are initiated to 'conquer' obesity, once and for all.

Before you shrug your shoulders and exclaim that, in that case, there is no use in trying, take a moment to think about what your extra weight means to you. In Chapter One I mentioned that being overweight had long-term health implications. For instance, if you are more than 10% over your ideal weight you are more likely to suffer from hypertension, cancer, diabetes, high cholesterol levels and coronary heart disease. All of these are major killers in the West and other, minor, diseases may also afflict the obese person. These include varicose veins, respiratory problems and joint problems in the lower back, hips and knees. In addition, being obese or very overweight is known to contribute to feelings of depression, inadequacy, guilt and embarrassment. You are more likely to feel that others are more beautiful, more worthy, more disciplined and so on, leaving your self-esteem at its lowest level.

The physical, mental and emotional consequences of obesity are clearly very serious indeed. And perhaps you can see that together these consequences can act to immobilize you and prevent you from taking any corrective action. Yet that is precisely what you must do if you wish to break this vicious cycle. *To reduce your weight you must commit yourself to making a gradual but permanent change in your diet and lifestyle.* There really is no other way.

For most people, this means losing about 1½–2 pounds a week on a diet of about 1,200–1,500 calories a day for women and 1,500–2,000 calories a day for men. This is a gradual, but effective, approach to weight loss. 'Starvation' diets consisting of much lower calorie intakes may not be safe, and in any case, the most sensible approach to weight loss is to begin with a medical check-up to make certain that you have no special health problems.

While making slow but important changes in your diet and lifestyle may not sound to be the most exciting or immediately rewarding decision to make, it is the *only one that will bring you lasting benefit*. If you don't believe this, let me give a few examples of other diet and weight-loss programmes that are available for the desperate dieter – and in order to follow some of them, you'd have to be *really* desperate.

APPETITE SUPPRESSANTS

Many drugs have been sold to dieters over the years to suppress their cravings for food. Amphetamines were used for some time as effective appetite suppressants, until their addictive potential began to be discovered. Even for those desperate (or stupid) enough to risk the side effects, there's still one major problem – when you stop taking them, your appetite becomes positively ravenous again. In some countries, drugs closely related to amphetamines are still sold for this purpose – phenylpropanolamine is one such drug, with very disturbing side-effects, especially when taken in conjunction with other drugs (or even with a cup or two of coffee).

In some countries, too, the local anaesthetic benzocaine is sold as an appetite suppressant. The idea, presumably, is that the anaesthetic effect of benzocaine 'numbs' the taste-buds on your tongue, and thus decreases your appetite. Unfortunately, the drive to eat comes not from your taste-buds, but from part of your brain called the hypothalamus, and the idea of swallowing significant amounts of a local anaesthetic (especially over a prolonged period) in order to quell your urge to eat is positively grotesque. Drugs? Just say *no*.

BANDAGES

This technique is like something out of *The Revenge of the Mummy* and it is marketed as if it were from Ancient Egypt, too. What happens is that two or three people get you to strip off while they soak metres of cotton bandages in some mysterious mud-like substance. Then they wrap you from neck to nether region to the knuckles of your toes and leave you lying on a bed while it dries! You are promised loss of several inches around each of those areas of body that all of us keep an eye on. Waist, hips, midriff, thighs and upper arms are all capable of triggering neurosis in most people, especially women over the age of 25. What really happens is that you lose water. When you are unwrapped from the bandages you are immediately weighed and measured around those crucial places. Of course you weigh lighter and measure smaller – until you go home and have a much deserved drink.

Bandaging treatment isn't cheap and it isn't 'medically recognized' either, as is often advertised. The only medical recognition it has, to my knowledge, is that of doctors trying to have it stopped.

CIGARETTES

Anyone who is seriously thinking about taking up smoking in order to lose weight must be absolutely stark, staring mad. While smokers sometimes put on some weight when they quit (they tend to eat more as a compensation for their lost habit), there is no evidence that the reverse is true. The only way you'll get slimmer by smoking is by contracting lung cancer – and that is a little drastic, don't you think?

DIURETICS

If you take a diuretic which makes you lose water from your body, then you'll obviously weigh less. Unfortunately, you'll also put the weight right back on again the next time your body ingests fluid. So the weight loss is very, very temporary. If you take a diuretic constantly, you're playing around with your body's chemistry, and it may not like it one little bit. You could get hooked – your body may learn to adapt to diuretics so successfully that it becomes accustomed to them, and insists that you keep taking them just to keep your weight down. Or you could seriously dehydrate yourself, leading to heart and kidney failure.

BULKING AGENTS

Food replacements such as fibre, methycellulose or guar gum are sold and prescribed in order to 'fill you up'. But recently, guar gum has been under suspicion, because there are fears that it could cause dieters to choke. Apparently, it could swell up in the throat and rupture the oesophagus. Not very pleasant, is it? And, of course, just filling yourself up with bulk isn't going to re-train your appetite.

LOW, LOW-CALORIE DIETS

All very low-calorie diets work, because they put your body into a state of semi-starvation (giving you as few as 300 calories in total). Poor body. Weight loss in this state can be very rapid indeed. But pause to consider – is the diet *also* supplying you with all the essential nutrients you need? Some of these diets have been shown to have undesirable side-effects – some have even been associated with sudden death. Personally, I wouldn't even consider going on such a brutal diet without having strict medical supervision at all stages (from my doctor, not from an 'advisor' who's really trying to sell me their products). But really, the biggest drawback to diets such as these is that they *don't re-educate your appetite*. Even if you successfully complete an arduous course of treatment, you're very likely to revert to your old ways of eating (maybe as a kind of reward) when you've finished. And then, just watch those pounds creep back on. Very disappointing indeed – except for the diet manufacturers, who can go on selling you their next diet . . .

FAD DIET BOOKS

There is big, big money to be made out of fad diet books. Unfortunately, this particular author won't be ordering a diamond ring on the strength of the book you're reading now, because *this* book is being as honest as possible with you, and not trying to sell you the latest diet craze. Basically, any diet that makes unreasonable claims, restricts you to an extremely narrow choice of food, or which doesn't help you to decrease your calorie consumption and increase your calorie expenditure (exercise) is probably not worth buying. Read it, if you like, as a work of fiction, but don't be fooled.

ARTIFICIAL SWEETENERS

The whole idea of using an artificial sweetener is to fool your stomach into believing that you're using sugar when you're really using another substance with fewer calories. So there is no genuine attempt to fundamentally change your way of thinking about food – you're really encouraging yourself to go on as before. The usefulness, therefore, of artificial sweeteners is actually less than the advertisements would have you believe. A number of artificial sweeteners have also had significant question-marks raised about their long-term safety. Don't be fooled into making them the centre-piece of your dieting effort.

SURGERY

Yes, some poor unfortunate people actually have themselves operated on in an attempt to reduce their fatness. Intestinal bypass surgery has been practised in Great Britain and, according to the surgeon responsible, with some success. Apparently 220 patients over a five-year period lost an average of 35% of their original weight. But before you consider this as an option, think about the side-effects. Diarrhoea. Malabsorption of nutrients from foods (when you've bypassed a huge section of your intestines, it's no wonder that they can't absorb vitamins and minerals properly). Potassium, magnesium and calcium loss. Kidney stones. Rheumatoid arthritis. Serious liver damage. No – this isn't an option *I'd* consider for one moment.

LOSING WEIGHT NATURALLY

I hope you agree that most of these examples are nothing short of brutal. They are physically intrusive and can damage your mental or emotional state. When you are in such a vulnerable position, the last thing you need is to be conned or abused. Yet

I suspect that the reason why diets and treatments such as those described above are continually lucrative is that the unfortunate dieter has not thought through the alternatives.

A natural weight-loss programme, one that relies on a collaboration between your personality and your body, is the obvious solution to excess weight. Losing weight naturally allows you a reasonable length of time in which to reduce. After all, you took a long time gaining your weight, why should you expect to lose it instantly? By losing weight naturally you will develop new eating patterns, new attitudes towards the food you eat – and both of these take time. Only then will you experience permanent weight control, a healthy, safe commitment that makes you feel better in more ways than any advertisement could ever promise.

CHAPTER FOUR
Your Diet For Life

There's no point at all in plunging headlong into yet another diet regime, only to emerge sadder but wiser a few weeks later, having lost little weight and more convinced than ever that 'it can't be done'.

Now wouldn't it be wonderful if there was a diet that could not only reduce your weight, but was also easy to follow, and one which you could adopt as your life-long pattern of eating? Wouldn't it also be a tremendous bonus if this diet decreased the likelihood of you suffering from diabetes, certain cancers, cardiovascular disease and rheumatic disorders? Well, there *is* just such a way of eating and it isn't new – it has actually been followed by thousands of people all over the world for several decades now. In fact, most of the diets that follow in this book are based on its principles.

This diet achieves these life-enhancing characteristics because it is very simple and highly versatile. There are no gimmicks, no expensive courses, no special high-protein drinks. Just lots and lots of good, wholesome food that is tasty, colourful and inexpensive. Want to hear more? In one sentence then – *just eat natural foods.*

The first question you're bound to ask is 'What does "natural" mean?' As a word, 'natural' has been distorted to the extent that it seems to have little meaning left. Almost everything you see in the supermarket seems to be classified as 'natural' by the manufacturers. So what – exactly – do we mean when we talk of a 'natural diet'? Here are some straightforward guidelines.

FOODS TO AVOID

Those containing additives, flavourings and colourings. Food colourings are used simply to make otherwise unattractive food more enticing – not for any good nutritional reason. Some of them have been linked to hyperactivity, birth defects, and others to tumours and cancer. In Britain 58 different colours can be legally used, six of which are not permitted in the EEC. One expert – Dr Erik Millstone of Sussex University – believes he has identified 25 chemicals, permitted as food additives in Britain, which may pose a significant toxic hazard to the population. Scientific studies highlighting possible dangers have been suppressed by successive governments for 20 years.* Some preservatives and anti-oxidants may also produce severe adverse reactions. The best advice is to avoid them.

FOODS TO CUT DOWN ON

Meat and Animal Products

Most meats and animal products, such as milk and cheese, are high in saturated animal fat – bad for your diet and bad for your health. Meat is often contaminated with antibiotics, hormonal substances, and other drugs that don't have to be shown on the label. Scientists have shown that people who don't eat meat suffer far less from cancer, heart disease, diabetes, hypertension, and other diseases. New problems associated with meat consumption are emerging all the time – such as bovine spongiform encephalopathy (sometimes called BSE), or 'cow madness', which is a *completely new disease* only recently discovered in Britain.

However, a few meats are less 'unhealthy' for those of you who might find a complete embargo difficult to enforce. In general, the redder the meat, the more saturated it is – beef, lamb and pork. Veal is a white meat, but often its rearing methods are 'intrusive' and unpleasant to many. Any red meat eaten should be trimmed well of any visible fat, and cooked in a way that will leach out as much fat as possible (grilling, see below).

White meats are generally considered to be less damaging to health and weight in that they contain very much less saturated fat. A good free-range chicken, its meat simply cooked, and with its fatty skin removed, should satisfy those who demur at the thought of a completely meat-free diet.

* Food Additives Campaign Team press release, 27 January, 1988.

The thing to remember is to *cut down* your intake – 115 g (4 oz) instead of 170 g (6 oz) per portion, for instance – and cook it in a healthy way with lots of vegetable or salad accompaniments to fill you up and give you a maximum of benefit.

As for milk, cheese etc. there are good alternatives, which you will encounter. If you find it difficult, however, choose skimmed milk, low-fat natural yogurt, low-fat spreads (you really *must* avoid butter and cream) – and low-fat cottage cheese or Quark. Instead of that ounce of hard cheese as a snack, chew on a carrot!

Fish and Fish Products
Fish has been sold as something of a 'health' food recently, with the discovery that certain types of fish oils can lower cholesterol in the blood. However, these oils can also be supplied from plant sources (if you're interested, flax oil is twice as strong in omega-3 as fish oil). What is often forgotten is that the pollution of our seas is at a peak with untreated sewage, and contamination from heavy metals (mercury, cadmium, lead, zinc – and sometimes plutonium, strontium, etc). Fish frequently show signs of disease, parasites and intestinal worms. And increasingly, fish taken from fresh and salt water are shown to be in a cancerous state. Not exactly the healthiest food, is it?

Again, however, fish *can* be wholesome and fresh, and if you select carefully, it may be included in a weight-loss diet. Oily fish, of course, are the 'fattiest', but the oil contains Vitamin D, which is vital in the diet (and only otherwise obtained from sunshine and some meats and dairy foods). White fish are those which store the fish oils in the liver – cod liver oil, for instance – and their flesh is much less fatty than that of oily fish as a result.

Choose carefully, cook just as carefully, and reduce the amounts consumed just as above.

FOODS TO CONCENTRATE ON

Fresh foods
Anything that has been artificially preserved isn't fresh. Some preservatives are known to cause cancer, others are suspected

of provoking allergic reactions. In today's world, where the 'shelf-life' of foodstuffs is often the uppermost concern in the manufacturer's mind, it is often very difficult to avoid food which has not been preserved to some extent. But even so, be discriminating, and try wherever possible to choose food which you know to be freshly prepared – or fresh (fruits and vegetables). This will mean changing your shopping habits, but it will be worth it.

Whole foods
Whole food is food which hasn't been interfered with. It hasn't been processed any more than is absolutely necessary to make it good and nourishing to consume. For example, polished and refined white rice is not nearly as wholesome as brown rice – which contains more protein, B group vitamins, and minerals (as well as tasting much better). Highly processed food is also bad for your diet because it is usually higher in sugars and simple carbohydrates, which give you more calories without the stomach-filling 'bulk' of fibre. Fibre is important (only obtainable from plant foods) because it will encourage your body to flick off the 'eat' switch much earlier – as soon as your stomach feels full, you'll naturally stop eating. And the easiest and most nourishing way to fill your stomach without breaking your diet is by eating plenty of fibre-rich foods.

A NATURAL FOOD DIET

A natural food diet includes all food in the main food-groups of vegetables, grains, fruits, seeds, nuts, pulses, legumes, yeast and soya products. There is obviously a great variety of food here – more than anyone could reasonably expect, in fact. Look at the vivid and colourful display of goods at a local greengrocers and you will see 50 or 60 different food items, and this number increases when the grocer supplies Indian, Chinese or Jamaican specialities. And in any supermarket or whole-food shop the range of grains, nuts, legumes, pulses and seeds is increasing as foods in these groups are re-introduced into common use.

All of these foods can be very easy and quick to prepare, and many of them may be eaten raw with little more than a wash to prepare them. Indeed, most of the foods you will eat on a natural food diet may be eaten raw. With a few exceptions (such as cooked pulses), raw food is nutritionally richer than its cooked counterpart and often has much more flavour. Buy organically grown foods when possible, especially fruits and vegetables.

But to show how to keep the cooking and preparation time to its absolute minimum, here are a few guidelines for utensils and cookery methods that will speed up your natural food diet preparation, without adding fats or robbing your food of its health-giving properties.

Cooking Utensils
There are five utensils that are very useful for making the change to healthy cooking. No others are needed to make this change, and, indeed, you may have the steamer or pressure cooker already. However, I will take this opportunity to recommend that you gradually eliminate your stock of aluminium pans – unless they are enamel-coated. Aluminium is known to be toxic to the human body and, unfortunately, pans made from this metal have recently been shown to pass some toxicity into the foods they cook. Instead, use stainless steel, enamel-coated, glass or iron pans. (Iron pans actually increase the amount of iron in your diet.) Non-stick pans are also recommended, especially as they help reduce the quantity of oil needed in cooking.

- A food processor is a versatile piece of equipment that speeds up most natural food preparation. A wide range of processors exist, costing anywhere from £25–£150. Each offers a set of blades and attachments that slice, dice, mix, purée, shred and grate in less time than it takes to talk about it. They are noisy and do need cleaning afterwards, but they also enable you to produce a salad, sauce or pâté in a matter of minutes.
- A blender is a large jug with a blade attachment in the bottom that sits on an electric motor. It may come with your food processor but, if not, I recommend you get one for those nut milks, milk shakes and even some of the dips and sauces you will be making. (They also make very good vegetable soups.) The depth of the jug means that you can make a very liquid mixture without worrying about it spilling over the centre opening – as can happen with some food processors. I also find that

my blender is slightly better at chopping nuts than my food processor.

• A universal steamer is a perforated basket whose sides are made of adjustable leaves of metal or plastic so that it may fit any pan. It is placed in a pan which contains little water. The vegetables (and fish or meat occasionally) are placed in the steamer, the pan is covered and the whole is placed over the heat. Steaming is an alternative to boiling vegetables: it is as quick as boiling but leaves more of the flavour and nutrition in your food.

• A juicing machine is quite magical – it transforms whole fruits and vegetables into their essential juices very, very quickly and neatly. The juice comes out one opening, the bulk goes into a separate container. You can drink the juice immediately, without lumps, and then go and empty the bulk on your compost heap. These are noisy and do need careful cleaning, but I wouldn't be without one.

• A pressure cooker is a quick and efficient way of cooking beans and pulses while retaining their nutritional value. Food is cooked with very little water in a sealed pan so that the steam created is kept under pressure. Vegetables may also be cooked in this way, although the saving in time is not nearly so great as when cooking beans. A stainless steel pressure cooker is preferable to an aluminium version and will cost several pounds.

Cooking Methods

The way you cook your food is often as important to its ultimate nutritional value as the type of food you buy in the first place. Many cooking methods cause great loss of nutrients and some methods even turn a healthy food into an unhealthy one.

• Steaming, using a universal steamer, as described above, cooks your vegetables quickly but without losing nutrients or texture. For instance, broccoli, cauliflower, carrots and even potatoes retain their colour, shape, 'biting' texture and flavour – all the qualities that used to end up in the water they were boiled in. (Chicken and fish can be successfully steamed as well.)

• Sautéing is often crucial in order to bring out the aroma and flavour of onions, garlic, some vegetables (and some meats), and it will be used in several recipes. However, two distinct forms of sautéing are recommended.

In the half sauté method, a maximum of only 15ml (1 tbsp)

of oil is used. The oil must be one of the oils high in linoleic acid, such as sunflower, safflower, corn, soy or olive. It should be measured into the pan and heated over a medium to high heat (not smoking or spitting) before the foodstuff is added. Stir the food constantly, adding other foods as per the recipe. Keep the heat high until the juices from the foods are released into the oil. Then reduce the heat and add any liquid etc. that is required. This method ensures the quality of flavour and aroma desired from a sauté, as well as the reduction in fat needed for health.

The New Sauté method does not use oil but still achieves the flavour, aroma, texture and nutritional quality desired from the sauté stage of cooking. Instead of oil, a very small amount – usually 15–30ml (1–2 tbsp) of liquid is heated in the pan until it bubbles furiously. The liquid may be water, stock, tomato juice, vinegar, gravy broth, diluted yeast extract or, indeed, any liquid you wish to use. Once the liquid is heated, the food is added and stirred constantly over a medium to high heat. As the food is more likely to stick in this method, the sauté time is not so long and the heat is slightly higher than in the oil sauté.

• Frying – cooking foods in quite a lot of oil – is not recommended.

• Boiling is used for rice and beans, and some sauces and soups may be brought to the boil before reducing them to a simmer. However, boiling is not used to cook vegetables as it greatly reduces their nutritional value, and may cause them to lose texture, colour and flavour.

• Grilling greatly reduces or eliminates the use of oil and fat in cooking. It also rids some meats and fish (if you're planning to include them in your diet) of a proportion of their fat content.

NUTRITIONAL VALUE

Using foods as advised above, you ensure that you derive a high level of nutrition from your diet – especially if you buy fresh fruit and vegetables that are organically grown. One of the most important aspects of safe weight loss is ensuring that your nutrient intake is kept high. This means selecting foods for their vitamin and mineral content, preparing them in a way that will retain their nutritional quality, and avoiding bad foods and habits (such as smoking) that will rob you of these very same nutrients. Then, your health is enhanced. Too often dieters cut down on *everything*, including the essential vitamins and minerals. Yet these substances are entirely calorie-free and are the backbone to good health.

Here are a few guidelines as to where to find your vitamins and minerals. Foods which are less natural, but which do have *some* goodness, are listed in parentheses.

Vitamin A	Yellow and dark-green fruits and vegetables (fish liver oil, cooked liver, cheddar cheese and eggs)
Vitamin B	Yeast, whole grains, legumes, nuts, molasses, dark-green leafy vegetables, root vegetables, soy beans, peanuts, sesame seeds, sunflower seeds, pumpkin seeds, wheatgerm, plamil Soya Milk (offal such as liver and kidneys, some meat and fowl, some fish, cheese, eggs and milk)
Vitamin C	Citrus fruits, rosehips, melon, strawberries, tomatoes, sprouted alfalfa, green peppers, broccoli (liver)
Vitamin D	Fortified plamil soya milk, sunshine (some fish, some dairy products)
Vitamin E	Whole grains, molasses, dark-green leafy vegetables, sweet potatoes, vegetable oils (liver, some dairy products)
Calcium	Dark-green leafy vegetables, molasses, legumes, almonds (milk, cheese, yogurt, fish)
Iron	Dark-green leafy vegetables, molasses, dried fruits, fermented soybean products (liver, kidney, eggs)
Magnesium	Whole grains, molasses, nuts, dark-green leafy vegetables
Phosphorus	Nuts, whole grains, legumes
Potassium	Whole grains, dried fruits, legumes, fresh vegetables, sunflower seeds
Zinc	Mushrooms, soy beans and soy-bean products, yeast, pumpkin seeds, sunflower seeds

WEIGHT LOSS FEATURES

So far we have a simple diet that is convenient, full of variety and very nutritious. But how will it help you to lose weight? To answer clearly, you will need to compare this diet with one that contains non-natural foods. Let us make this comparison in three parts, dealing with fat, protein and carbohydrates in both diets.

Fat

In a diet based on non-natural foods the average intake of fat is 40% of the total calorie intake and, often, more than half of this fat is of the saturated type. Saturated fat is known to create cardiovascular problems such as hardening of the arteries, thrombosis and heart attack. Gaining 40% of your calories from fat is unwise, unhealthy and unnecessary. This figure should be reduced to a *maximum* of 30% and, preferably, an even lower 20–25% of your total calorie intake.

If your total calorie intake is currently 2000 calories per day, and if you are one of those 'average' people who derive 40% of these calories from fat, then you are eating fat to the value of 800 calories per day. Although fat is an essential part of your body and your diet, this amount is excessive. If it is not converted into energy then it will be stored as body fat and you will *gain weight*. A simple means of controlling your intake, one that arrives at a very healthy percentage of total calories, is to *cut your fat intake in half*. Here's how:
- Eliminate animal fats from your diet as much as possible.
- Alter your cooking methods to exclude those using a lot of fat – frying, for instance.
- Replace animal cooking fats with cold-pressed, organic vegetable seed oils. These include soya, olive, safflower and sunflower oils. While these oils may be more expensive than those labelled simply 'vegetable oil', they are more flavourful and you will need to use much less to achieve the taste and 'body' desired in your meal. In fact, why not experiment with the more exotic oils such as walnut and sesame so that your appreciation of 'good fat' becomes a hallmark of your cooking.
- Use moderate amounts of margarines such as Granose and Vitaquel.
- Use these oils and margarines only when you will be able to

taste them. If they will be lost in the other flavours of the meal, don't bother using them.

As you know, saturated fat is known to contribute to cardio-vascular disease. Most saturated fat is derived from animal foods with only a very little included in plant foods such as palm and coconut (so avoid them, and products which contain them). All the plant oils mentioned above are low in saturates, and additionally contain more of vitamins A and E when purchased as cold-pressed oils. They also contain linoleic acid – a fat that your body needs and which must be gained in your diet. Linoleic acid is essential to the health of *all* cells, the transportation of oxygen and to healthy glandular function. It also works to keep the arteries clear and flexible – quite the opposite to saturated fat!

The majority of the diet programmes in this book are based on the recommendations listed above because a high-fat diet is not compatible with a weight-loss diet. In fact, it is not compat-ible with a healthy diet, no matter what your weight. A *little* fat in your diet is important, but it must be represented in moderate quantities and in a healthy form if you are to avoid the risks from cardiovascular disease and obesity.

Protein
'But where do you get your protein!?' This is the sound of what I call 'protein anxiety', a condition suffered by many people in which a great deal of unwarranted emphasis is placed on the importance of protein in the diet. Let me put a few myths to rest.

First, protein is present in every living thing. You have protein, I have protein, cows have protein, beans have protein, broccoli has protein. So the first myth, that all protein must come from meat or dairy produce, is unfounded.

The second myth is to do with 'complete' and 'incomplete' proteins. There are twenty-two amino acids which combine in various ways in your food. However, your body can actually produce fourteen of these amino acids itself, only the remaining eight must be supplied in your diet. These are called 'essential amino acids'. By eating a variety of whole, fresh foods, your body is able to organize all twenty-two amino acids itself – even if some of them are made in your body, some come from baked beans (oh yes, baked beans *can* be part of a natural diet) and the others from brown bread. In other words, you don't *need* to eat animal proteins, because your body will combine all the amino acids it receives from a good variety of food to make its own completion protein.

You only need enough protein to build new tissue and repair old tissue, about 10–12% of your total calorie intake as protein. (NOTE: Pregnant or nursing women, please see note at the beginning of the book, also, if you are badly injured, with broken bones and torn muscles, it is possible that you would require more protein than this. Please consult your doctor.)

When you eat too much protein, more than is needed for tissue building and repairs, the extra protein is converted by your liver into fat. This conversion is one that places unnecessary stress upon your liver and, anyway, that fat is stored away just like all your body fat and is only 'redeemable' as energy. You do yourself no favours by following a high-protein diet. In a natural food diet, protein is available in large quantities in:

beans	lentils	grains
nuts	seeds	potatoes
soya milk	tofu (bean curd)	tempeh (fermented bean cake)

Carbohydrates

Carbohydrates are the cornerstone of a natural food diet and, in effect, you will be following a high-carbohydrate, high-fibre diet. If you recall, carbohydrates can be simple, such as sugar; or complex, such as potatoes. A simple carbohydrate does not include complex carbohydrates and so it supplies 'instant' energy (and little else) to your body. Any surplus is stored as fat.

Complex carbohydrate, on the other hand, does contain simple carbohydrate – but it also contains starches and fibre. This means that it provides a package of three services. As a complex carbohydrate breaks down, it supplies a little instant energy (simple carbohydrate) to your body. It doesn't stop there, however, because there is more to break down. As the starches (complex carbohydrate) break down, more energy is supplied to your body, but this energy is produced in small amounts over a period of time. Taking time like this means you feel more satisfied for longer and your body isn't placed under stress trying to find the energy it needs. Finally, when all the energy is derived from that complex carbohydrate item, you are left with fibre – an indigestible matter that, nonetheless, works for you to improve your health.

Fibre moves through the digestive system and, as it does so, helps to transport fats, vitamins and minerals. It helps to keep the intestinal walls elastic and 'clean' and absorbs lots of water so that your bowel movement is made much easier. Complex carbohydrates and fibre are good for you! Don't listen to anyone who tells you that baked potatoes or whole wheat bread are fattening. They are wholesome, nutritionally valuable, and they may help you to lose weight – but only if you don't smother them in butter, gravy and soured cream!

In a natural food diet simple carbohydrates will be minimized in favour of complex carbohydrates. Many natural foods supply simple carbohydrates and these may be enjoyed without worry. However, the simple carbohydrates derived from refined foods are less healthy and should be avoided. They are usually high in calories, low in nutrients and stressful for your body to cope with. This means that the list of foods on the left should be eliminated or greatly reduced from your diet, while those on the right may be taken freely (F) or in moderation (M).

sugar	molasses (M)
sweets	fresh fruits (F)
chocolate	carob (naturally sweet, caffeine-free alternative to chocolate) (M)
squash	unsweetened fruit juices (F)
sugary snacks	dried fruit (unsugared) (M)
jam	unsweetened preserves (M)
sweetened breakfast cereals	muesli with soya milk or fruit juice (F)

Complex carbohydrates should comprise 65–70% of your total calorie intake. Here is the good news about complex carbohydrates.

• They are bulky foods, so you never feel empty.

• You are less likely to overeat when following a high-complex carbohydrate diet – its bulk means that it takes a long time to chew!

• They break down slowly and provide you with a steady trickle of energy (simple sugars) over a long period of time.

Whenever the occasion, whatever you want to say, send your message with a beautiful bouquet from Flying Flowers, the UK's favourite postal flower company.

Every time you send **FLOWERS FOR CHARITY with Flying Flowers, quoting our special order reference ICR/9697/A they will donate at least 15%** of the total value to our funds, so always quote ref. ICR/9697/A.

TO ORDER: COMPLETE THE COUPON BELOW AND POST WITH PAYMENT OR FAX (CREDIT CARD PAYMENTS) TO 01534·865554 (24 HRS). ALTERNATIVELY TELEPHONE 01534·865665 (8am-6pm 7 days) quoting ref ICR/9697/A (to ensure donation is paid) and order details.

IMPORTANT NOTES: BOUQUETS MARKED * NOT AVAILABLE FOR CHRISTMAS DELIVERY. CHRISTMAS ORDERS REQUIRED NO LATER THAN 10TH DEC. DELUXE CHRISTMAS BOUQUET CONTAINS 15 ASSORTED RED SPRAY & BLOOM CARNATIONS WITH 2 GOLD EUCALYPTUS (FOR NOV./DEC. DELIVERY ONLY).

Registered in Jersey No. 2044. Flying Flowers Ltd, Retreat Farm, St. Lawrence, Jersey, C.I.

- -

PRIORITY ORDER FORM Prices valid until 31.3.97   ICR/9697/A

MY NAME _____

ADDRESS _____

_____

_____ POST CODE _____

DAYTIME TEL NO. _____ Please send bouquet indicated	CODE	PRICE	TICK	FLYING FLOWERS WILL DONATE
12 Luxury Carnations	12 FFC	£9.99		£1.50
5 Freesia, 5 Carnations, 5 Spray Carnations	15 FFC	£12.99		£2.00
* 10 Spray and 8 Bloom Carnations *	18 FFC	£14.99		£2.25
* 22 Asst. Carnations & Gypsophila (illust.) *	22 FFC	£16.99		£3.00
Deluxe Christmas Bouquet	15 XMR	£14.99		£2.50

TO: NAME _____

ADDRESS _____

_____

_____ POST CODE _____

MESSAGE (max 10 words) _____

_____

_____

Delivery required by ___ /___ /___ or by Christmas ☐

I enclose cheque/PO for £_____ payable to Flying Flowers or debit my

Access/Visa card no. | | | | | | | | | | | | | | | | |

Expiry Date _____ Signature _____

Post with payment to FLOWERS FOR CHARITY, FLYING FLOWERS LTD, PO BOX 473, JERSEY, JE4 9WE. Registered in Jersey No. 2044. Flying Flowers Ltd, Retreat Farm, Jersey, C.I. Although despatched by 1st class post to arrive by the required date the exact day of delivery cannot be guaranteed.

- When selected for their freshness and wholeness (unrefined), they supply you with most of the vitamins and minerals you need for good health.
- These vitamins and minerals are taken in the doses and combinations which nature intended, because you are eating the foods whole and as close to their natural state as possible.
- The high-fibre aspect of these foods ensures that your body functions better, assimilating more nutrients and moving waste through your body more efficiently.
- The high-fibre content of complex carbohydrates means that fewer calories are derived from these foods.

It is important to mention that recommending potatoes isn't the same as recommending chips! A food that is a complex carbohydrate in its natural state, may become a manufactured item that bears little or no resemblance to its authentic form. Let's use potatoes as an example of the do's and don't's of preparing complex carbohydrate foods.

Potato DO's	Potato DON'T's
baked	fried
steamed	with soured cream
sautéed in olive oil	with butter
in soups	crisps
mashed	pommes anna

You can see that the best way of preparing this wonderful food is to leave it quite free of fats. Where fat is used, it is a minimal amount of the type recommended earlier. Similar lists could be drawn up for other foods, emphasizing fat or sugar as the undesirable ingredient. The 'bottom line' then is how you treat the food. If you prepare it to retain as much wholeness, nutritional value and flavour as possible, then you are more likely to benefit from the food's inherent quality. The recipes listed later in this book may, I hope, give you some inspiration in this style of cooking (even those containing meat and fish). There are wonderful sauces, dressings and dips included that can be used to top *any* of the basic complex carbohydrate foods, just to prove that healthy food need not be dull food. Here is a short list of staple complex carbohydrate foods for you to welcome into your kitchen:

whole wheat bread	whole grain rice	whole wheat pasta
potatoes	root vegetables	leaf vegetables
fresh fruit	sun-dried fruit	millet
barley	oats	rye
cous cous	nuts	seeds
beans	lentils	chickpeas

WHAT'S NEXT?

The above is the framework on which the majority of the diets in this book are formed. Its key features are that it is incredibly simple, exceptionally healthy, and an easy and comfortable way of life. To comply with this basic diet, the following factors must be observed:

● Your intake of animal produce is reduced as much as possible.

● Your daily basal metabolic calorie needs are met from whole, fresh food.

● Preservatives, colourings and other rubbish are avoided.

● Fat is reduced to 20–25% of your total calorie intake.

● Complex carbohydrates are increased to 65–70% of your total calorie intake.

However, each one of the diets in the following chapters deals with the issue of weight loss in a slightly different manner so that, while all of them will help you lose weight, one or more of them might suit *you personally* better than the others. For let's face it, we are all different, and it really would be impossible to create a diet programme that would suit all people. You have your own way of thinking, your own routines and patterns of work. You might like to lie in bed till nine each morning and party every Friday night, while your dearest friend might go swimming every morning at six and hibernate with a good book at weekends. Yet both of you might wish to diet! She might work in industry, you might be a librarian – how is it possible to say that what is right for her is also right for you? I don't think it is possible.

A natural food diet is a permanent, life-long change in your eating habits and, hopefully, your eating perception. I know that it works for those wishing to lose weight and I know that it can grace you with those other health bonuses I've mentioned.

But, I also know that you may need little shoves or pulls now and again. You may need 'breaks' or a change in routine or even a really good fast. You may even find it difficult to break away completely from your old 'bad habits', and thus I have interspersed some recipes which use some chicken, fish, cheese and eggs. These *do not* form part of what I call a natural food diet, but they demonstrate how you can cut down on animal products while, at the same time, increasing your intake of more natural foods. Always accompany main course dishes with lightly cooked vegetables or a good salad.

Following are nine diets which each offer a unique angle on weight loss and which, collectively, provide you with a set of versatile routine-breakers that will keep you interested, successful and, most of all, positive about the new commitment you have made towards reducing your weight and eating a diet that is well and truly for life.

CHAPTER FIVE

The Liquids Only Diet

Many people need a 'kick start' into a weight-loss programme. They need to feel that they are making a definite, even drastic, change in their diet, and they need to notice its effects immediately. The liquids only diet can meet these needs. It is brief (a maximum of three days), interesting, and an effective means of preparing your body and your brain for a new way of life.

This diet is the only programme in this book that comes near to being a fast. It gives you the calories and satisfaction you require, but it doesn't have the bulk – or the chewiness! – of the other diets included here. However, it does have rather special benefits and effects. The liquids only diet is of the type that has recently been called a 'cleansing' or 'de-toxifying' diet. It works by reducing the amount of solid matter you consume and replacing it with highly nutritious beverages. Because these beverages are light, easy to digest and fairly undemanding of you in general, your body is able to perform its natural waste-removing functions more easily, and more rapidly. Without the immediate addition of more substantial foods, the process of excreting toxic waste is perhaps more thorough during this diet – it is certainly more noticeable and more profound than usual! For example, it is likely that, in following the liquids only diet, you will experience a day or two of bad breath, a feeling of your tongue being coated, or you might develop a spot or two on your face or back. These are the natural side effects of a profound release of waste material, or toxins, from your body.

Of course, your body is always releasing toxins from your system. As your tissue cells die they are carried away in your lymph and excreted from your body while other, new cells replace them. As your food is digested, the by-products are pushed through your system, certain of which are waste, and they too are excreted. Even as you breathe you exchange waste material for oxygen-rich air. So releasing toxins is nothing new for your body, it is an essential part of good health. But if the excretion of waste material is sluggish or insufficient, health problems can result. Pain, stiffness, tension, headache and constipation are but a few of the discomforts which you may suffer yourself, and each of these can be at least worsened, if not caused, by poor excretion.

Your body has four means of excreting toxins from your body: through exhalation of breath, through perspiration, through defaecation and through urination. In addition, the protective membranes of your body, such as those in your mouth, nasal passages, lungs and throat, are capable of increasing the amount of mucous produced to prevent external toxins from invading and also to help remove those already present in your system.

When you exchange your usual diet for the liquids only diet you allow your body to increase its rate of de-toxification because it is more readily able to discard toxins that have accumulated over a period of time. Especially if you had followed a meat or dairy-based diet, you may find that the change in how you feel is very noticeable. This is because a diet based on animal produce takes longer to digest than does a plant based diet and any food substance, plant or animal, that stays too long in your system will produce a surfeit of waste material. So switching to food that moves through you more rapidly will also ensure that waste matter is excreted more rapidly. Those who have tried the liquid only diet use very vivid imagery to describe its beneficial effects: 'like a spring clean', 'I felt a lot of junk had been flushed out of my body', 'at the end of it, I felt new'.

You will lose some weight on this diet because, although it weighs heavy with water, it contains very little fat – only that naturally present in the foods you are juicing. It is also surprisingly high in fibre and exceptionally high in vitamins and minerals. So given that it is only used for a maximum of three days you should see and feel some very satisfying results. However, before you think of it as an 'instant' weight loss programme (which it most definitely isn't) let me reiterate that its main purpose is to invigorate and cleanse you, to make you feel eager and prepared for a new dietary way of life and to make you feel *better*. This little diet may be used as either a starting point or an 'interval' to other diet programmes. You may repeat it occasionally to help you adjust to jet lag, overcome the 'blues', finish off a long-term cold or prepare yourself for an important meeting or event. Here are its summary features:

- use of nutritious liquids only
- for a maximum of three days, a minimum of twenty-four hours
- repeated at intervals of no less than seven days
- to cleanse, invigorate and prepare your body for dietary change
- to promote initial weight loss

The vitamins and minerals essential for your good health are amply supplied in this programme through the consumption of juices made from raw fruits, nuts or vegetables. The juices are easily digested. Improved health of your mucous membranes, digestion and the elimination processes follow naturally from this diet.

Most of the juices mentioned may be purchased in bottled form. In this case, however, it is important to purchase only unsweetened and unadulterated juices – the Biotta brand is an excellent choice. However, it is worthwhile purchasing a juicing machine and/or a blender if you intend to use this programme on a regular basis. They make the juicing process quick, inexpensive and very easy – and there is nothing to match a *very* fresh juice for flavour, aroma and nutritional value. Fruits, nuts and vegetables selected for juicing should be grown organically if possible – without chemical sprays or fertilizers. If you are uncertain about the growing conditions of the foods you select, put extra effort into washing or peeling them.

THE DIET OUTLINE

- Upon waking, drink a cup of hot water with the juice of half a lemon stirred into it. Lemon juice helps with digestion, elimination and weight loss and replenishes Vitamin C in the body. Take the lemon juice dilution first thing in the morning, before you get out of bed if possible.
- For breakfast, select another fruit juice, such as apple, cherry, strawberry, or a combination of these. Drink at least 570 ml (1

pint) of this juice slowly. If you prefer, you may drink 285 ml (10 fl. oz) of fruit juice and the same amount of a vegetable juice such as tomato, carrot or beetroot.

- For a mid-morning snack, drink at least 285 ml (10 fl. oz) of any fruit juice, or of any nut milk (see recipe section).
- For lunch, drink a vegetable juice such as celery, carrot or beetroot. Some people prefer to combine these vegetables in juice form – this is acceptable and very tasty. However, any vegetable juice is suitable at this time. Other fruits and vegetables may be made into a 'cocktail' to suit your taste. Drink at least 570 ml (1 pint) of juice at this time.
- For a mid-afternoon snack, drink at least 285 ml (10 fl. oz) of any vegetable juice, or of any nut milk (see recipe section).
- For the evening meal, drink at least 570 ml (1 pint) of vegetable juice or 285 ml (10 fl. oz) of any nut milk (see recipe section).
- At bedtime, drink a final 285 ml (10 fl. oz) of fruit juice or any nut milk (see recipe section).
- In addition, drink as much herbal tea or mineral water as you desire. You may make tasty and nutritious cocktails by combining various fruit and vegetable juices listed below.

FRUITS

Apple
Rich in Vitamin C, malic acid and a selection of minerals. This juice disinfects the digestive tract, prevents constipation and detoxifies the liver. A good juice to prevent complications in your health. Four large apples make approximately 570 ml (1 pint) of juice.

Cherry
This juice acts on the digestion, liver and kidneys to clear uric acid from the body. Remove the stem and the stone before juicing. 450 g (1 lb) cherries makes approximately 285 ml (10 fl. oz) of juice.

Citrus
Oranges, grapefruit and lemons come into this category, all are rich in Vitamin C, and all have a cleansing effect on the intestines

which prevents bowel disorders and problems with elimination. However, avoid grapefruit if you suffer from an ulcer or colitis. Orange and grapefruit are best taken diluted just before a meal. Lemon is the best juice to use on a regular basis as an early and mid-morning tonic.

Grape

High in iron and Vitamins A, B and C, this juice is naturally sweet and therefore can be taken alone, in large quantities, over one or two days without causing weakness or loss of health. It prevents over-acidity in the body and helps in all forms of elimination and detoxification. 450 g (1 lb) grapes makes approximately 285 ml (10 fl. oz) of juice.

Strawberry

Rich in Vitamin C and high in iron and calcium, this fruit makes a light and tasty juice. Strawberry juice is useful in cases of anaemia as its iron content is presented in combination with other nutrients to make the iron easy for the body to assimilate. Anaemia is very common if you are suffering an infection. In addition, this is simply a delicious fruit juice and a very pretty one too. 450 g (1 lb) strawberries makes approximately 450 ml (15 fl. oz) of juice.

VEGETABLES

Beetroot

This juice is full of minerals that are presented in a way which makes them easy for your body to absorb. It removes toxins from the blood, increases your red blood cell count and can even reduce fever. It can also correct a tendency to suffer from constipation. Beetroot juice may be combined with carrot or celery juice to enhance both its flavour and its healthy effects. 450 g (1 lb) of beetroot makes approximately 570 ml (1 pint) of juice.

Carrot

If you select the deep orange-coloured carrots in preference to the pale orange, this juice can provide a very large quantity of Vitamin A. Vitamin A benefits all of your glands, keeps all your mucous membranes healthy and helps you develop a clear skin. 450 g (1 lb) carrots makes approximately 570 ml (1 pint) of juice.

Celery
This juice is rich in minerals which have a soothing effect on the nerves and a stimulating effect on your major organs. It has a mild diuretic effect, thus speeding the removal of toxins from your body. One head of celery makes approximately 450 ml (15 fl. oz) of juice.

Cucumber
Juice the whole of the cucumber, including the skin. It is valued for its mild diuretic effect and high potassium levels. One large cucumber makes approximately 285 ml (10 fl. oz) of juice.

Dandelion
It is difficult for most people to find fresh, unpolluted dandelion leaves, but those who can should add the leaves to other vegetable juices. This plant has diuretic properties but, more importantly, it is rich in Vitamin A, calcium, magnesium and potassium.

Lettuce
This plant is exceptionally rich in minerals and is a useful addition to your favourite vegetable juice. The outer, darker leaves, though often less attractive, are more nutritious than the pale, inner leaves. Choose Cos lettuce in preference to iceberg or Webb.

Parsley
Parsley is good as an addition to other vegetable juices, adding a clean, earthy flavour and a high Vitamin A and mineral content. It freshens the breath and is a mild diuretic.

Tomato
This juice is easily digested and supplies many of the essentials for general good health. Vitamins A, B, C, D, and E are available in tomato as are many minerals and trace minerals. Of course, fresh, raw and organically grown tomatoes are by far the most nutritious and tasty. This juice may be drunk by itself or mixed

with other plants to make a juice cocktail. 450 g (1 lb) of tomatoes makes approximately 450 ml (15 fl. oz) of juice.

Watercress

Add this to other juices or use it by itself in a dilution of mineral water. It is rich in minerals and helps to remove toxins from your body.

NOTE: Do not mix grape juice with carrot juice, or citrus juices with watercress juice.

All fruits and vegetables for juicing should be well washed and trimmed of stalks. Fruits such as apples and grapes may be juiced without peeling or removing the seeds, but the juice may need to be strained before drinking, according to your taste. Vegetables such as carrots and beetroot need only have the woody tips remove before cutting into manageable pieces and juiced.

See the recipe section for:
Fruit Juices, Herbal Teas, Mint and Citrus Drink, Nut Milk, Simple Almond Milk, Vegetable Juices

CHAPTER SIX

The Raw-Food Diet

Some of the healthiest and longest living peoples in the world thrive on a predominantly raw-food diet. The Hunza, a people who live high in the Himalayas, eat a diet of nearly 70% raw foods and they are purported to be a culture 'without disease'. In this country as well, a raw-food diet has been popular for generations as a way of improving and maintaining health. There are two main benefits in following a raw foods diet. First, toxins are removed from the body rapidly and thoroughly while the abundance of vitamins, minerals and trace elements present in raw food are quickly assimilated by your body. And second, the raw-food diet epitomizes the low-fat, high-fibre diet that is also nutritious and low in calories. Therefore it is easy to lose weight in this programme without worrying about undernourishment.

You may begin this diet immediately you have completed the liquids only diet, or you may start it immediately you decide to begin losing weight. In either case, be prepared for a continuation of the detoxification of your body. Unlike the liquids only diet, the raw-food diet is one that may be followed for four to six weeks without change, if desired. Here is a basic set of guidelines for your safe and successful use of this programme.

• Plan your starting date, preferably in a week when you are not expected to go out to eat or to prepare an especially traditional meal for others. As the starting date approaches, do your best to clear temptation – in the form of pre-cooked or processed food – from your refrigerator and cupboards.

• Replace this food with raw fruits and vegetables, purchasing your supply daily to ensure maximum freshness. When possible, buy organically grown produce to minimize the quantity of pesticides and other chemicals you take in with your food.

FOODS TO INCLUDE

- Any raw, fresh fruit.
- Raisins, sultanas, prunes, figs, dates and other dried fruits, *provided* they are sun-dried.
- Any raw, fresh vegetable (you *can* eat raw beetroot, turnip and cauliflower). Vegetables which need cooking, such as marrow, or that you do not find attractive in their raw state, should not be purchased.
- Raw, whole grains – such as oat flakes, barley flakes, wheat bran and wheat germ. These may be mixed with fruit to form a cereal such as muesli, or sprinkled over a bowl of fruit to add bulk and vitamin value.
- Raw nuts and seeds. Avoid the roasted, dry roasted or heavily salted selections available, and it is a good idea to avoid peanuts if this is the first time you have tried a raw-food diet. Instead, purchase raw nuts rich in Vitamin B, such as Brazil, almond, cashew, pistachio, walnut and filbert, and seeds such as sunflower, pumpkin, sesame, caraway and poppy. These are all tasty and nutritious with high vitamin and mineral values.
- Cold-pressed olive, sunflower or safflower oil.
- Unsweetened fruit and vegetables juices.
- Herbal teas and mineral waters.
- Organic apple cider vinegar.

FOODS TO AVOID

- All animal produce.
- Bread, cakes, biscuits, crackers and pastry.
- Tinned and frozen foods and highly processed products such as breakfast cereals and snack foods.
- Sweets, chocolate, ice creams.
- Coffee, tea, cocoa, milk drinks, alcohol.
- Soya milk, tofu and tempeh.
- Any cooked or processed vegetables and fruit.
- Dried fruits which are not sun-dried – ask your shop-keeper.
- Rice, millet, cous-cous, barley and all grains needing to be cooked.
- Salt and sugar.

• Vegetable oils that have been heat processed – if they don't say 'cold-pressed' on the label, you should probably avoid them.

You may be surprised to realize just how much of the food you normally consume is cooked in some way. In fact, it is possible that you may feel a little 'lost' at first and wonder what you *can* eat. After the first two or three days, however, you will realize that the raw food diet is an abundant one. While you are following it, you should *eat as much food as you like*. Don't go hungry! Just make sure that all the foods you eat are *completely* uncooked and of the best quality you can find.

What improvement should you expect? Well, for a start, your food will taste better, you will have more energy and your mood will be brighter – all within the first week of this programme. People who have maintained a raw food diet for more than two weeks have reported improvements in their general health and, of course, a definite reduction in their weight. I recommend that you follow this diet for four to six weeks to achieve the cleansing process as well as a significant drop in your weight. By the end of six weeks you should know whether or not the diet suits you. If you are happy with it, then by all means continue as you are! If you feel you need a change of pace, a little variety, then try one of the other diet programmes recommended in this book. At all times, however, adhere to the natural food diet, simply explore the various diet options here to keep your interest up and your weight down!

Here is a list of recipes, included in the recipe section, that you may use in the raw food diet.

Country Cabbage Salad, Gardener's Salad, Herb and Tomato Salad, Minty Fruit Salad, Simple September Salad, Fruit and Fennel Sauce, Herb and Garlic Dressing, Hot Mustard and Chilli Dressing, Cornucopia Melon, Fruit and Nut Muesli, Fruit Juices, Mint and Citrus Drink, Nut Milk, Simple Almond Milk, Vegetable Juices

CHAPTER SEVEN

The Nine-Day Diet

This programme is for those who find it easier to follow a more formal diet, for longer than two or three days, as a way of edging into a new diet lifestyle. It is also an ideal programme to follow before starting a new job or when going through some other form of change in your life. The nine-day diet is divided into three distinct phases and, as well as enabling you to enjoy an initial weight loss, will help to alter your taste for food. Often your sense of taste is the primary cause of weight gain, with the flavour of salt, sugar or fat governing all your food choices. Like the liquids only diet, it is intended for use over a brief period of time (nine days) and may be repeated at intervals to keep your weight down. If you should decide to repeat it, leave an interval of six weeks between starting dates, during which time you may try one or more of the other programmes described here.

In this diet it is important that you do not limit your intake of the foods recommended. It is not a diet in which you need to count your calories, except to ensure that you do not undereat. If you are hungry, eat! But only the foods that are recommended for that phase of the diet. Please weigh yourself at the beginning of the diet, and again at the end of the nine days.

PHASE ONE

The first, second and third days of this diet are intended, like the liquids only diet, to help you eliminate waste and boost your level of energy. You may experience some of the side effects of a rapid 'cleansing' of your system, such as a bad taste in the mouth and possibly one or two spots on the face or back.

During this phase, eat as much food as you like, do not 'calorie count' and eat a variety of those listed during any one day. I recommend that you have a minimum of 2.25 kg (5 lb) of fresh fruit, 900 g (2 lb) of dried fruit, and a variety of juices available at all times. Here are the foods to eat during phase one:

- Any raw, fresh fruit.
- Any unsweetened fruit juice.
- Any sun-dried fruit.
- Any unsweetened vegetable juice.
- Any herbal tea.
- Any nut milk (see recipe section).

PHASE TWO

The fourth, fifth and sixth days of this diet are used to boost your intake of vitamins and minerals. Also in this phase, the bulk of food you consume increases. As before, do not worry about counting calories; instead, put your efforts into selecting foods that are fresh and organically grown if possible. Here are the phase two foods:

- Any or all of the foods from phase one.

plus

- Any raw vegetables.
- Any raw grains – such as flaked barley, oats, wheat germ or bran.
- Any raw seeds – such as sunflower, pumpkin, sesame, poppy.
- Any raw nuts – such as almond, cashew, walnut, hazelnut, pecan.
- Cold-pressed oils – such as sunflower, safflower, olive or sesame, up to 3 tablespoons per day.
- Organic cider vinegar – up to 3 tablespoons per day.

This collection of foods actually give you a great deal of scope for preparing very substantial and interesting meals. Here is a suggested menu on which to base your meal preparation, followed by a list of suitable recipes to use from this book.

Breakfast	Unsweetened apple juice
	Raw food muesli with unsweetened fruit juice
	Herb tea
Mid-morning	Fresh fruit, any amount
	or
	115 g (4 oz) of mixed dried fruit and nuts

Lunch	A fresh salad weighing at least 450 g (1 lb) to consist of at least one food from each of these groups: Green leaf, raw root, seed, nut or berry, stalk or bulb, flower, and dressed with a cold-pressed oil and fresh lemon juice or apple cider vinegar.
	Fruit juice, herb tea or mineral water
Mid-afternoon	Fresh fruit, any amount
	or
	115g (4oz) of mixed dried fruit and nuts
Evening Meal	A fruit salad
	A fresh salad weighing at least 450g (1 lb), as above
	Any fruit or vegetable juice or nut milk

Here are a selection of recipes included in the recipe section which are suitable for this phase of the diet programme:

Country Cabbage Salad, Gardener's Salad, Herb and Tomato Salad, Minty Fruit Salad, Simple September Salad, Fruit and Fennel Sauce, Herb and Garlic Dressing, Hot Mustard and Chilli Dressing, Cornucopia Melon, Fruit and Nut Muesli, Fruit Juices, Mint and Citrus Drink, Nut Milk, Simple Almond Milk, Vegetable Juice

PHASE THREE

Finally you may use the seventh, eighth and ninth days of this diet to return to a more 'normal' meal pattern. In this phase, cooked foods are allowed but they are selected for their nutritional values and their ability to sustain you in a healthy eating pattern. So no returning to chocolate bars, beef steak and chips – after six days of 'clean living' you may have lost your taste for those foods in any case. And, having come this far, you should find that the taste and aroma of these phase three foods are far better and more inviting than you remember them.

- Any or all of the foods from phase one *and* phase two *plus*
- Baked potatoes
- Steamed or boiled whole grain rice

- Tofu (soya cheese)
- Tempeh (fermented soybean 'meat')
- Steamed or boiled whole grains and pulses – such as barley, millet, cous-cous, oats, lentils and beans
- Wholewheat bread – fresh or toasted, without margarine or jam
- Soya milk
- Organically produced wine – such as those from the Alsace region of France, one glass per day, if desired

Here is a sample menu on which to base your meals:

Breakfast	Fresh fruit, any amount Muesli with fruit juice or soya milk *or* Toasted whole wheat bread with sugarless preserves, no margarine Fruit juice, herbal tea or mineral water
Mid-morning	Herbal tea, fruit or vegetable juice Raw fruit or vegetables, any amount
Lunch	A fresh salad weighing at least 450g (1 lb) to consist of at least one food from each of these groups: green leaf, raw root, seed, nut or berry, stalk, bulb or flower, dressed with lemon juice and including chopped tofu or wholewheat pasta. One slice of whole wheat bread Herbal tea, fruit or vegetable juice Up to 285 ml (10 fl. oz) nut milk
Mid-afternoon	Herbal tea, fruit or vegetable juice Raw fruit or vegetables, any amount 55g (2oz) mixed nuts, seeds and dried fruit
Dinner	Fruit or vegetable salad starter Light soup or broth Cous-cous with steamed broccoli *or* Baked potatoes filled with baked beans *or* Brown rice and lentil sauce (Dhal) *and* Steamed carrots or greens

Sugarless cake or hot fruit soup
Herbal tea or mineral water

And here is a list of recipes included in the recipe section which are suitable for this phase of the diet programme:

Cabbage and Red Bean Salad, Chinese Tofu Marinade, Cinnamon Porridge, Cooked Brown Rice, Cooked Whole Wheat Pasta, Cornucopia Melon, Country Cabbage Salad, Creamy Walnut and Onion Salad, Crunchy Pasta Salad, Fruit and Fennel Sauce, Fruit and Nut Muesli, Fruit Juices, Gardener's Salad, Herbal Teas, Herb and Garlic Dressing, Herb and Tomato Salad, Hot Fruit Soup, Hot Mustard and Chilli Dressing, Hot Scandinavian Salad, Lemon Bean Salad, Lentil Soup, Lunch-Box Marinade, Milky Carob Drink, Mint and Citrus Drink, Minty Fruit Salad, Nut Milk, Onion and Olive Dip, Orange and Sweet Potato Bake, Parsley Potato Salad, Pea and Tofu Purée, Simple Almond Milk, Simple Dhal, Simple September Salad, Smooth Lentil Pâté, Special Spuds, Spicy Banana Milkshake, Split Pea Soup, Tangy Tempeh Marinade, Vegetable Juices

WHAT'S NEXT?

When you have completed the nine-day diet, compare your weight with your record of your previous weight. Here I want to offer an immediate word of support: it is possible that the weight difference will be slight. In most people an encouraging amount of weight is lost in this diet; in a few people, however, the weight loss is less than they might have hoped.

You may recall that earlier I said that in order to be successful in reducing your weight, you must commit yourself to a permanent change of diet. In effect you must change your life. Don't let this sound daunting, however. Nine days is just the beginning, the most rewarding time is still about to happen to you. So if your weight loss has been minimal, remember that it is just the very early stages of a turning point. You may not have lost pounds and pounds, but your body has already begun to change a great deal.

On the tenth day, that is, immediately after you have completed this diet, begin another of the diet programmes included in this book. It is possible that at some point you may wish to repeat this nine-day diet and you should feel free to do this at your whim, though allowing six weeks between starting dates is best, as I've already mentioned. As you learn about the other diets, you will realize that you can rotate programmes to alternate more formal with more relaxed meal patterns. Always select the diet programme that will suit your personal and social needs at that time, but maintain a natural food diet as though your life depended on it. Certainly the quality of your life does!

CHAPTER EIGHT
The Macrobiotic Diet

If you are overweight and also suffer from chronic disorders or disease such as hypertension, rheumatism, skin problems or constipation, you may benefit from introducing the macrobiotic principle to your natural food diet. This encourages you to treat your food as a healing influence in your life, and can have far-reaching effects as there are layers of understanding you may acquire about the foods you eat and how they affect you.

The guiding principle in macrobiotics is the presence of two forces – yin and yang – present in all things and which complement and balance one another. So, for any concept or description you encounter, there is an equal but opposite concept or description. The macrobiotic principle contends that these opposites are, in fact, always part of the same entity, that together they create a unity and balance that is health-giving and providing insight into the meaning and processes of life.

Based on ancient oriental philosophies, the yin-yang concept has been popularized in the West, applied to food and given the name 'macrobiotics' by Mr Georges Ohsawa. Macrobiotics advocates a diet of in-season, whole foods which have been grown locally. The staple food of the macrobiotic diet is grain – rice, barley, wheat, rye, oats and millet – which makes up at least 70% of the macrobiotic diet. Pulses and lentils are also important, as are seaweeds and local fruits and vegetables, which, however, are consumed in much smaller quantities than are normally recommended. Extreme foods are avoided: sugar (extreme yin), and salt and meat (extreme yang), are examples of such foods. At a glance, this diet is not very different from a natural food diet.

A macrobiotic diet can begin to undo the errors of a life of poor or inadequate diet by re-establishing a balance in your body to give you a background of health which improves as the diet becomes a way of life. You gradually gain an understanding and confidence which enables you to respond, through your diet, to the needs and demands of your life and your environment.

This understanding may be particularly valuable if you are overweight because of consistently over-eating or eating a poor diet. Often these errors are due to a basic misunderstanding of how your body works, how food is utilized, even how you fit into the world around you. The macrobiotic principle can help you to feel and observe the relationship between the various elements of your life clearly and calmly. You may then make active changes, to old perceptions of yourself and the food you eat.

Mr Ohsawa recommends a strict, ten-day diet for those starting a programme to reduce their weight. It is simple: for ten days eat only unrefined whole grains. You may eat them raw, boiled, steamed or baked. You may purée or cream them. Also, you may *eat as much as you like* provided you chew thoroughly. After ten days you may gradually add lightly cooked vegetables, soups and fruits until you arrive at a diet you are happy with.

This diet should not be repeated more than once every six months. To avoid confusion, please ensure that you eat *at least 450g (1 lb) of raw, whole grains each day* to meet your calorie needs. Prepare this grain in any way you like (except frying) and accompany it with a clear fluid intake. Use only a tiny pinch of salt in each cooked meal.

A less drastic diet, though most definitely macrobiotic, is one which Mr Ohsawa summarized,* in these five points:

1) Suppress sugar completely from your diet.
2) Learn that it is possible to live without being carnivorous.
3) Eat primarily whole-grain cereals, vegetables, beans and seaweeds – all as unrefined as possible.
4) Eat as little as possible of other foods.
5) Keep liquid [intake] down to a minimum.

Here is a list of recipes, included in the recipe section, which are suitable for this diet. Any combination of local, in-season foods may be prepared into raw or lightly cooked dishes and added to this list.

* *Macrobiotics, The Way of Healing*, Georges Ohsawa, 1981, Georges Ohsawa Macrobiotic Foundation.

Apple and Oat Cake, Chinese Tofu Marinade, Cinnamon Porridge, Cooked Brown Rice, Hot Fruit Soup, Nut Milk, Simple Almond Milk, Simple Dhal, Spicy Carrot Sauté, Tangy Tempeh Marinade

SEA VEGETABLES (SEAWEED)

In addition, the sea vegetables that are available in most whole-food shops may be included in any quantity in macrobiotic cooking. These are very rich in minerals and vitamins, very low in fat and high in fibre. Here is a summary of the most common types.

Arame
This is a delicate, lacy vegetable with a very mild flavour, not at all 'fishy'.

Agar
This is the vegetable form of gelatine and is used to make jellies and other dishes that need a setting substance. It is very high in fibre and usually comes in powdered form, so it is easy to use. Agar (also called agar-agar) will not work when there is vinegar, chocolate, spinach or rhubarb in the dish, but it will usually set a dish at room temperature.

Dulse
This seaweed is chopped, then soaked, then added to soups, stews, stir-fries and casseroles where it adds a definite chewy texture. Dulse has an exceptionally high iron content and is very rich in magnesium and potassium. 56g (2 oz) is sufficient in a dish for four to six people.

Irish Moss
Also called carrageen, this is a very commonly used sea vegetable. Like agar, it is often used to make jellies or other dishes that need to set. It may be used successfully with those foods, such as spinach, rhubarb and chocolate, that do not work well with agar.

Nori

This is another delicate and versatile sea vegetable, most famous for its use in sushi. You may buy nori shredded or in sheet form.

Kelp

So famous for its nutritional value that it is sold in tablet form for those wishing to increase their mineral intake. You may buy it in powdered form and add one or two tablespoons to a sauce or casserole.

Kombu

I don't actually *eat* kombu, but I do use a strip in every soup or stew I make because it adds nutritional value, as well as gently thickening the liquid part of the dish. Once the dish is made, I remove the kombu because it has done its work.

CHAPTER NINE

The Fast-Food Diet

Don't get too excited! This doesn't mean that chips and beef burgers are suddenly 'in', nor that a back-slide into cream buns and sugary tea is about to be encouraged. No, in simple terms this diet is for those who are, by nature, nibblers! If you would rather snack your way through the day than sit down to a blow-out meal, this diet is for you. Or if you find that, appealing though a blow-out meal might sound, you still get hungry between meals, again – this could be your diet.

The formula for the fast-food diet is that you eat six to eight times per day, ensuring that each fast feast is calorie controlled as well as adhering to a natural food diet. This style of eating may be beneficial for those who get moody, headachey or tired between meals, and it is often suitable for those who would eat between meals in any case – even though they are already well-fed.

● Women following the fast-food diet should eat six to eight snacks per day, each one comprised of 150–200 calories, increasing to 250 calories per snack when the desired weight loss is achieved.

● Men following this diet should eat six to eight snacks of between 200 and 250 calories each, increasing to 300 calories per snack when the desired weight loss is achieved.

● No more than two snacks per day should be the same to ensure that a great variety of food is eaten.

An important element of this programme is the speed and attention with which you eat. Please allow at least 10 minutes per snack, more if possible, and while you are eating, *just* eat! Chew your food well and give it time to settle before you start rushing around again.

This programme may be used over a long period of time because it includes a variety of foods and may be altered to meet your calorie requirements. It is important to change to another diet form, however, if you find yourself either over-eating at each fast-feast time, or eating the right amount at each snack but no longer eating a sufficient number of snacks. This would mean that you weren't getting enough calories. Another pit-fall is to eat full-sized meals as well as snacking four to six times per day. You have to be firm on this point: *either* full-sized meals *or* snacks, not both! That way lies weight gain.

When you prepare each of the snacks you will enjoy in one day, be at your most creative and wrap or display them in the most attractive way you can manage. This little detail will help you to slow down and contemplate the food you are eating. The trouble is, snacks are so often gulped or 'wolfed' down, with little time for your taste buds to work, much less for artistic appreciation. Taking your time about eating will also give your stomach a chance to signal the 'off' switch on your appetite. Just allowing a minimum of 10 minutes to each meal will give your body a chance to say 'No, I've had enough, thank you'. Once that happens, you are on your way to a re-trained appetite.

Here is a list of recipes, included in the recipe section, that are suitable for the fast-food diet. All of them measure 300 calories or less per portion. Please see the individual recipes for precise calorie values.

Apple and Oat Cake, Bubble and Sprouts Savoury, Cabbage and Red Bean Salad, Carrot and Coriander Soup, Celery and Potato Soup, Celery Soup, Chickpea and Onion Soup, Chinese Tofu Marinade, Cooked Whole Wheat Pasta, Cornucopia Melon, Creamy Walnut and Onion Salad, Country Cabbage Salad, Fruit and Fennel Sauce, Fruit Juices, Gardener's Salad, Greek-Style Spinach, Herbal Teas, Herb and Garlic Dressing, Herb and Tomato Salad, Hot Fruit Soup, Hot Mustard and Chilli Dressing, Hot Scandinavian Salad, Hot Tempeh Take-Away, Lemon and Peanut Sauce, Lemon Bean Salad, Lentil Soup, Light Vanilla Oat Cake, Lunch-Box Marinade, Milky Carob Drink, Mint and Citrus Drink, Minty Fruit Salad, New Mexico Chilli, Onion and Okra Stir-fry, Onion and Olive Dip, Orange and Sweet Potato Bake, Parsley Potato Salad, Pea and Tofu Purée, Sharp Tomato Sauce, Simple Dhal, Simple September Salad, Slightly Sweet Tomato Sauce, Smooth Lentil Pâté, Special Spuds, Spicy Banana Milkshake, Spicy Carrot

Sauté, Split Pea Soup, Stuffed Pumpkin Bake, Sweet and Sour Spaghetti Sauce, Tangy Tempeh Marinade, Tea-Time Toast and Jam, Thick Broccoli Soup, Tomato and Tofu Soup, Vegetable Juices, Whole Wheat Bread

Plus any amount of raw vegetables.

CHAPTER TEN
The King, Prince, Pauper Diet

For some people, breakfast is the most crucial meal of the day. Perhaps they work hard in their sleep, fighting off weird nightmares or solving mysterious cosmic riddles. Whatever the cause, the need these people have for a hearty breakfast is real – it is not a whim of their personality but a definite physical requirement. Others, of course, feel exactly the opposite about breakfast, often preferring to avoid it entirely. In this programme, however, I outline a day's diet that starts with a growl and ends with a purr. Our grandmothers used to say 'Breakfast like a king, lunch like a prince, supper like a pauper' to describe a sturdy, yet healthy, daily diet pattern. The thought behind this pattern was to feed heavily when that food would be immediately put to good use, rather than eat heavily when all you would be doing after the meal was sleeping.

This programme may be used indefinitely provided a natural food diet is adhered to and your calorie intake does not exceed your needs. With that provision, I add a word of caution: some people find that, having started the day like a king, they also want to *end* it like a king! If you slide into this pattern, stop this programme immediately and switch to another diet in this book.

It is impossible to set exact calorie limits for each of the three daily meals in this programme, but roughly speaking you should aim to eat half your calorie requirements at breakfast, slightly more than one quarter at lunch and slightly less than one quarter at the evening meal. The difference between the lunch and evening meals should manifest in the lightness or digestibility of the food. For instance, soup and salad is an excellent evening meal because it is filling but does not require strenuous effort to digest. It will keep you happy, but not drowsy, throughout the evening and let you wake up ravenous. The luncheon meal should supply you with the energy you need for the rest of your working day, without leaving you feeling sleepy and sluggish the entire afternoon. Please adjust the calorie content of each meal to suit yourself, however, You may well find that, to feel at your best, breakfast takes on feast proportions, with lunch and supper thinning down to mere snacks.

Here is a menu listing recipes, included in the recipe section, that will comply with the king, prince, pauper diet.

King's Breakfast	285 ml (10 fl. oz) any fruit juice
	Herbal tea or mineral water
	with one of the following:
	Cinnamon Porridge
	Fruit and Nut Muesli
	Sunday-Best Mixed Grill
	Tea-Time Toast and Jam *with* Cornucopia Melon
Prince's Lunch	285 ml (10 fl. oz) any nut milk *or* any vegetable juice
	Any soup *or* any salad
	with one of the following:
	Big Burgers
	Hot Tempeh Take-Away
	Special Spuds
	Bean Cheese Whip and Biscuits
Pauper's Supper	285 ml (10 fl. oz) any fruit juice
	Herbal tea or mineral water
	Any soup
	Any salad
	Hot Fruit Soup
Plus, all day	Any amount of mineral water, herbal tea, vegetable juice or raw fruit

CHAPTER ELEVEN

The Weekend Diet

All right, so you're not very overweight – only ten pounds or so – but you would really like to lose that weight. The trouble is, you are also a working person expected to have generous business lunches and boozey Happy Hours with clients and colleagues. If you start announcing 'I'm on a diet' to all and sundry, you will get blamed for lowering morale – not surprising if most of them carry a few too many pounds, too! How can you lose weight on the quiet?

The answer is surprisingly simple, but I must caution you that this diet is not designed for those who wish to lose more than 1 stone (14 lb) in weight. It is for those who are moderately overweight and are, to some extent, unable to follow a regular, controlled diet programme during the week. Here is how the weekend diet works.

MONDAY TO FRIDAY

Follow natural food diet from Monday to Friday, quietly and without worrying too much about calorie intake. Instead, over these five days you should aim to select foods that have an obviously lower calorie content than those you might be used to selecting. For instance, following a natural food diet you won't be eating steak and mushrooms, but something like Caesar salad with tagliatelle al pesto. The salad and pasta are lower in calories than the steak and mushrooms choice, just as filling and equally acceptable in your social setting. (You may, of course, be tempted to some sort of animal food intake – do choose something like plainly cooked fish or chicken.) If you can carry on in this way all week, you can lower your total calorie intake by something like 400 calories per day – without going hungry!

There are *always* alternatives to the high-fat, high-protein, high-calorie nonsense that is promoted in many restaurants. Here is how to learn about those alternatives:

• Ask the waiter what the restaurant can offer to suit your way of eating. You may do this at the restaurant or over the phone and, in either case, take your time and don't be put off if the waiter seems hesitant. If necessary, ask the chef or manager to provide alternatives. They can only say no, in which case you can find another restaurant.

• Look on it as an adventure. Buy a restaurant guide and make an effort to discover 'new' restaurants that are happy to provide sensible food without making you feel like a troublemaker.

• If you are being taken to a place you suspect won't have what you want on the menu, make up your own meal ahead of time and order it with confidence and authority. For instance, if your colleagues are taking you to a steak house, be prepared with something like this: 'I find I'm not really in the mood for a heavy meal today. Please bring me the fresh melon to start, followed by seasonal vegetables dressed with your mushroom and pepper marinade.' No one can argue with that!

• About those Happy Hours: once or twice a week might be important to your work, but every evening is pushing your luck. Apart from the health complications it can create, alcohol consumption is responsible – all on its own – for a great many cases of obesity. *Reduce your intake by slowing down, and by cutting down.*

The quantity of alcohol suggested as a *maximum* intake per week is: for men, 21 units; for women, 14 units.

One Unit =	285 ml (10 fl. oz) ordinary beer or lager
	1 measure (single) of any spirit
	1 glass of wine
	1 small glass of sherry
	1 measure of vermouth or aperitif

Remember, these are considered the maximum allowances for normal health. More detailed recommendations suggest that intake should be lower still for optimum health, and that two or three days in each week should be alcohol-free. In addition, the speed at which you drink should be reduced so that no more than one unit of alcohol is consumed per hour.

AT THE WEEKEND

As Saturday morning dawns, prop up on one elbow and down a dilution of the juice from one lemon and one cup of boiled water. Now continue as you started and spend this weekend following either the liquids only diet (page 44) or the raw-food diet (page 51). Very simple!

Should an opportunity occur for you to maintain your weekend diet for longer than the weekend, please take it. The liquid only diet is really intended for a three-day maximum; however, the raw-food diet may be continued for a longer period of time if the time is available. Or you might try the nine-day diet when you are certain you have that period of time free from your dining and drinking commitments. I recommend that you maintain the natural food diet even after you have lost your excess weight. It will guarantee that you keep it off.

CHAPTER TWELVE
The Nine-to-Five Diet

The most dangerous time of the day for many people trying to lose weight is that thirty-minute period when they arrive home from work. Imagine it for yourself – you have put in the required eight hours, travelled to and from the work place and now, at last, you arrive into the relaxed and familiar atmosphere of your own home. Naturally you want to sit down and quietly nibble something – just until you can summon the energy to make a proper meal.

Does this sound like you? If so, then the nine-to-five diet programme might be perfect for you. From the moment you get up in the morning until the moment you arrive home from work (or until five o'clock if you don't work), you follow the raw-food diet of Chapter Six. Once you get home, however, you simply follow the natural food diet. In other words, you can have your piece of cake at six o'clock providing it is high-fibre and low-fat. Then you can go on to have a lovely cooked meal with as many courses as you like – provided every single food complies with the requirements of a natural food diet, and provided you revert to the raw-food diet the next morning.

This programme has enabled many people to lose weight who have previously found it impossible to 'stick to a diet'. Many of them have found that they are more alert and energetic during their working hours as a result of eating only raw food during this time. And by following the natural food diet in the evenings, they know that they are still controlling their intake of fat, sugar and calories, even though they are eating a substantial and tasty meal. There is one question that is often asked however, and that is 'what about the weekends?' Well, you have several options. You may

- maintain this nine-to-five pattern of eating
- follow the natural food diet all weekend

- follow either the liquids only *or* raw-food diet
- try the king, prince, pauper diet

You may vary how you deal with the weekends, according to what social plans you have made. Remember, the whole point of offering you a range of diet programmes is so that you may be successful in losing weight. The natural food diet is the only constant; the other programmes offer you a way of matching this diet to your personality, your circumstances and your current social plans.

Here is a list of recipes, included in the recipe section, that are examples of foods you may eat before and after five o'clock.

BEFORE 5 O'CLOCK PM

Country Cabbage Salad, Gardener's Salad, Herb and Tomato Salad, Minty Fruit Salad, Simple September Salad, Fruit and Fennel Sauce, Herb and Garlic Dressing, Hot Mustard and Chilli Dressing, Cornucopia Melon, Fruit and Nut Muesli, Fruit Juices, Mint and Citrus Drink, Nut Milk, Simple Almond Milk, Vegetable Juices

AFTER 5 O'CLOCK PM

Any of the above
Any of the recipes included in the recipe section
1 glass of organically grown wine

One especially appropriate recipe for this diet is called the nine-to-five stew. You prepare it in the morning and leave it cooking at a very low temperature all day. You arrive home to the wonderful aroma of a hot stew, *and* it is ready to eat!

CHAPTER THIRTEEN
The Monday-to-Friday Diet

Weekends are for parties, extravagance and indulgence. Right? If you agree, chances are you will have difficulty following a diet programme in the midst of all that revelry. However, there is a way of achieving your desired weight loss without destroying the spontaneity and enjoyment of your weekend.

- Follow a liquids only diet on Monday.
- Follow a raw-food diet on Tuesday, Wednesday and Thursday.
- Follow the nine-to-five diet on Friday.
- Follow a natural food diet from Friday evening through to Sunday bedtime without counting calories (or indulge, if you must, in some meat or fish dishes, but strictly count your calories).
- Keep your alcohol intake to a minimum.

In other words, you keep the strict element of your diet programme confined to weekdays and, at the weekends, give way to your natural tendency to indulge. Notice, however, that I really recommend that a natural food diet is maintained throughout the weekend. Here I will reiterate that diet is a way of life, a permanent commitment to a style of eating that can either cause obesity, disease and disorder, or can establish vigorous health which leaves you looking and feeling well!

It is your choice which outcome you would like from your diet. You are the only person in control of what you put in your mouth. Hopefully this book has served to simplify some of the complex or obscured issues surrounding obesity and weight loss. More importantly, I hope that it has offered you a small handful of tools by which you may repair and rebuild your relationship with food, appetite and eating.

CHAPTER FOURTEEN
Helpful Weight-Loss Recipes

The majority of the recipes included here will make high-fibre, low-fat, low-sugar meals, and are free of animal products. Those which use animal products are as low-fat as possible and, although chicken or fish contain no fibre, their accompanying vegetables do in many cases. Eat these main-course dishes with lightly cooked vegetables or salads to gain maximum benefit. Each recipe is accompanied by a nutritional analysis which gives values for calories, total fat and fibre. These figures are taken from the Expanded Foods Database, Nutri-Calc Plus™.* They are based on nutritional analyses that are currently available, therefore many of the figures are approximate. The analyses are listed per portion, unless otherwise stated, i.e. Value for Whole Cake or Total Value. In these cases, divide the figures by the number of servings you decide the recipe will make. These recipes are listed in alphabetical order.

Apple and Oat Cake

Serves 4
Value Per Portion: Calories: 210.8
Total Fat: 6 gm   Fibre: 2.5 gm

2 tart apples
50 g (2 oz) whole wheat flour
115 g (4 oz) rolled oats
2.5 ml (½ tsp) ground cinnamon
1.25 ml (¼ tsp) ground cloves
5 ml (1 tsp) baking powder
285 ml (10 fl. oz) water
15 ml (1 tbsp) oil

* Based on nutritional figures from the US Department of Agriculture Handbook 8, and food manufacturers' analyses.

Warm the oven to 300°F, 160°C, Gas 3 and lightly oil a 20cm (8 inch) cake tin. Peel and finely chop the apples and mix them with the dry ingredients in a mixing bowl. Stir the water and oil together and pour this liquid into the dry mix. Stir well, adding a little more water if necessary to give a smooth, moist batter. Spoon the batter into the cake tin, spread evenly to the corners, and bake for 25–30 minutes. Cool for 15 minutes, then remove from the tin and cool on a rack.

Bean Cheese Whip and Biscuits

Serves 4–6
Total Value: Calories: 449.5
Total Fat: 23 gm   Fibre: 42 gm

285 g (10 oz) firm tofu
15 ml (1 tbsp) mild mustard
15 ml (1 tbsp) soya milk
2 spring onions *or* 15 ml (1 tbsp) chives, finely chopped
16 Matzos

Break the tofu into a blender, add the mustard and the milk, and purée to a smooth consistency. Add a little more milk for a softer cheese. Spoon the mixture into the serving bowl and add the finely chopped onion or chives. Stir well and serve immediately or chill for 30 minutes. Spread a little on each of the matzos. NOTE: A single cracker has only 17 calories and .05 grams of fat. Matzos are made without added salt or fat.

Big Burgers

Serves 4
Value Per Portion: Calories: 336.4
Total Fat: 12 gm   Fibre: 4.9 gm

4 vegetable burgers (only those which may be grilled)
4 whole wheat baps
115 g (4 oz) Cos lettuce leaves
2 tomatoes
½ cucumber
15 ml (1 tbsp) mild mustard

Grill the burgers according to the instructions provided by the manufacturer. Prepare the salad ingredients by washing, slicing and dividing into four servings. When the burgers are nearly ready, lightly toast the inside of each bap and spread one half with mustard. Place the burger in the bap, top with the salad ingredients and serve.

Bubble and Sprouts Savoury

Serves 4
Value Per Portion: Calories: 60.36
Total Fat: .8 gm   Fibre: 1.9 gm

5 ml (1 tsp) yeast extract
60 ml (2 fl oz) water
450 g (1 lb) Brussels sprouts
1 small onion, peeled
1 × 285 g (10 oz) can bamboo shoots
freshly ground black pepper to taste

Dissolve the yeast extract in the water. Wash and trim the sprouts and halve or quarter them. Chop the onion. Rinse the bamboo shoots under cold water and drain. Pour half the yeast into a frying pan and place over a high heat until it begins to bubble. Add the sprouts and onion and stir often for 5 minutes. Add the bamboo shoots and black pepper and stir gently together. Cook for another 5 minutes. Serve over rice, pasta or with other vegetables.

Cabbage and Red Bean Salad

Serves 4
Value Per Portion: Calories: 144.1
Total Fat: 4.6 gm   Fibre: 1.2 gm

450 g (1 lb) cooked kidney beans
225 g (8 oz) carrots, scrubbed
½ small head white cabbage
2 medium oranges
25 g (1 oz) slivered almonds

Ensure the beans are fully cooked (if they are canned, the label should say if cooking is necessary), and drain them into a large bowl. Shred the carrots and cabbage into the bowl. Peel and thinly slice the oranges and add them, with any juice, to the salad. Sprinkle the almonds over the salad and stir gently. Serve immediately.

Carrot and Coriander Soup

Serves 4
Value Per Portion: Calories: 13.9
Total Fat: 17 gm   Fibre: .5 gm

2 medium onions
2 medium carrots
2 litres (4 pints) water or vegetable stock
50 g (2 oz) fresh parsley
50 g (2 oz) fresh coriander
4 small bay leaves

Peel and thinly slice the onions. Scrub and grate the carrots. Heat a little of the stock in a large saucepan and, when it is bubbling, drop the onion in and stir constantly as in a sauté. When the onion is tender, add the grated carrots to the sauté and stir well. Gradually add the remaining stock, stir well and reduce the heat. Wash and trim the parsley and coriander, then chop them finely. Add the herbs and bay leaves to the broth and simmer, covered, for 20 minutes. Serve hot.

Celery and Potato Soup

Serves 4
Value Per Portion: Calories: 223
Total Fat: .5 gm   Fibre: 1.4 gm

900 g (2 lb) potatoes, peeled
2 medium onions, peeled
30 ml (2 tbsp) cider vinegar
5–10 ml (1–2 tsp) freshly ground black pepper
5 ml (1 tsp) caraway seed
1–2 litres (3–4 pints) water
5 stalks celery
3 bay leaves

Dice the potatoes then place them in a colander and rinse them under cold water. Leave to drain. Finely chop the onions and sauté them in the vinegar in a large, deep saucepan. Stir constantly over a medium flame. When the onions are soft, add the potatoes, pepper and caraway. Stir well then add the water and keep stirring for 1–2 minutes. Bring the soup to a low boil, reduce the heat and simmer, covered, for 20 minutes. Chop the celery and add to the soup. Add the bay leaves. Simmer for a further 10–15 minutes and serve.

Celery Soup

Serves 4
Value Per Portion: Calories: 75.63
Total Fat: 3.8 gm   Fibre: 1.2 gm

15 ml (1 tbsp) oil
2 medium onions, peeled
5 ml (1 tsp) caraway seed
1.5 litres (3 pints) water
1 head celery
1 bunch fresh parsley
juice of 1 orange

Heat the oil in a deep saucepan over a medium flame. Thinly slice the onions and sauté them until they begin to soften. Then sprinkle the caraway seed over them and continue to sauté, stirring constantly. Add the water, stir very well and increase the flame to bring the broth to a gentle boil. Meanwhile, wash, trim and chop the celery and parsley. When the broth has boiled, add the celery and parsley. Stir very well, cover the pan and reduce the heat. Leave covered and simmer for 10 minutes. Add the orange juice just before serving.

Chicken and Mushroom Salad

Serves 4
Value Per Portion: Calories: 117.4
Total Fat: 2.807 gm   Fibre: 1.322 gm

225 g (8 oz) cooked chicken, skinned
115 g (4 oz) button mushrooms, washed

225 g (8 oz) celery, trimmed and diced
a little Herb and Garlic Dressing (see page 90)
freshly ground black pepper
1 crisp lettuce
15 ml (1 tbsp) chopped parsley *or* snipped chives

Dice the chicken. Dry sauté the mushrooms in a non-stick pan for about 5 minutes, then cool. Mix together the chicken, mushrooms, celery, dressing and seasoning to taste. Shred the lettuce finely and make into nests on the serving plates. Heap the salad into the middle, and sprinkle with parsley or chives.

Chicken and Pepper Kebabs

Serves 4
Value Per Portion: Calories: 108.3
Total Fat: 4.903 gm   Fibre: 0.6 gm

15 ml (1 tbsp) olive oil
30 ml (2 tbsp) lemon juice
1 garlic clove, peeled and crushed
freshly ground black pepper
15 ml (1 tbsp) chopped fresh mint
3 small chicken breasts, skinned, boned and cut into 2.5 cm
    (1 inch) cubes
2 large green peppers, cored, seeded and cut into 2.5 cm (1
    inch) squares

Mix the olive oil with the lemon juice, garlic, seasoning to taste, and fresh mint. Pour over the chicken cubes in a shallow dish and leave, covered, for about 4 hours. Remove the chicken, and thread on to four skewers, alternating with the pepper squares. Brush with the marinade and grill under a preheated grill for about 5 minutes. Turn over, brush again, and grill for a further 4–5 minutes. Serve immediately.

Chickpea and Onion Soup

Serves 4
Value Per Portion: Calories: 256
Total Fat: 2.9 gm   Fibre: 3.6 gm

170 g (6 oz) dried chickpeas
450 g (1 lb) carrots
3 cloves garlic, peeled
2 large onions, peeled
1 × 425 g (15 oz) can chopped tomatoes
5 ml (1 tsp) freshly ground black pepper
1–1.5 litres (2–3 pints) water
1 strip kombu (seaweed, see page 63, optional)
15 ml (1 tbsp) cider vinegar

Soak, rinse and pressure cook the chickpeas. Scrub the carrots and slice in thin rounds. Finely chop the garlic and onions and 'sauté' them in a large saucepan using a little juice from the tomatoes. Add the ground pepper and carrots to the sauté and stir well. Gradually add the tomatoes and water and bring the mixture to a simmer. Add the kombu and the chickpeas and stir. Simmer for 30 minutes. Just before serving, stir in the vinegar.

Chinese Tofu Marinade

Serves 4
Value Per Portion: Calories: 78.59
Total Fat: 3 gm   Fibre: .6 gm

285 g (10 oz) firm tofu
140 ml (5 fl. oz) cider vinegar
25 g (1 oz) fresh ginger, peeled
a pinch of freshly ground black pepper
115 g (4 oz) button mushrooms

Cut the tofu into small chunks, place in a bowl and pour the vinegar over. Slice the ginger very thinly and add to the tofu; sprinkle the pepper over it and stir gently. Clean and quarter the mushrooms and add to the tofu, stir again, cover and leave to marinate for 2–4 hours. Serve cold or heat the whole mixture in a saucepan over a medium heat. Serve with rice, pasta or a salad.

Cinnamon Porridge

Serves 1
Value Per Portion: Calories: 582.8
Total Fat: 24. gm Fibre: 4.2 gm

50 g (2 oz) porridge oats
25 g (1 oz) raisins or sultanas
285 ml (10 fl. oz) soya milk
a pinch of ground cinnamon

Measure the oats, raisins and milk into a small saucepan and place over a low heat. Stir frequently as the mixture thickens and leave to cook for 7–10 minutes, adding a little water if necessary. Serve hot with a sprinkling of ground cinnamon.

Cooked Beans

Most beans double in bulk once they are cooked. To gauge how much you need for a meal, the rule of thumb is that 55–115 g (2–4 oz) of dried beans are enough for one serving, depending on what will accompany them. All beans must be well washed and well cooked to avoid indigestion.

Cooking Times

Chickpeas: Soak overnight. Cook for 30 minutes in the pressure cooker; 3 hours in the pot.
Kidney beans: Soak overnight. Cook for 30 minutes in the pressure cooker; 1½ hours in the pot.
Butter beans: Soak for 4–6 hours. Cook for 30 minutes in the pressure cooker; 1½ hours in the pot.
Soy beans: Soak overnight. Cook for 40 minutes in the pressure cooker; at least 3 hours in the pot.
Black-eyed beans: Soak 4–6 hours. Cook for 20 minutes in the pressure cooker; 1 hour in the pot.
Split peas: Wash them well. Cook for 1 hour in the pot.

Cooked Brown Rice

Serves 1
Value Per 340 g (12 oz)   Calories: 348
Cooked Portion:
Total Fat: 1.8 gm   Fibre: 1–5 gm

115 g (4 oz) raw whole grain rice
285–350 ml (10–12 fl. oz) water, approx.

Measure the rice into a mixing bowl and cover with cold water.
Now wash the rice by swirling your hand through it and exerting
a scrubbing motion. Drain the water and repeat this process
three times until the water is fairly clear. Drain the rice and tip
into an iron pot.

When cooking rice, the ratio of water to rice is generally 2/1
by volume.

Cover the clean rice in the pan with twice its volume in water.
Cover the pan and place over a high flame. Bring the water to
the boil, then reduce the flame as much as possible and leave
to simmer for approximately 50 minutes or until the water is
completely absorbed. Keep the pan covered while it cooks, only
lifting the lid at the end of the cooking time to check that the
rice is finished.

Don't stir the rice at this point, or it may become gummy. If
it is still too firm at the end of 50 minutes, add a little boiling
water to the rice. Cover again and cook for another 10 minutes.

Brown rice takes longer to cook than white rice because it is
a whole grain. However, it is more nutritious than white, refined
rice and has ten times the flavour.

Cooked Whole Wheat Pasta

Serves 1
Value Per 225 g (8 oz) Serving: Calories: 206.5
Total Fat: 6.4 gm   Fibre: 10–20 gm

water
50 g (2 oz) whole wheat pasta of choice

Bring a large pot of water to a hard boil and add the pasta to
it. Boil the pasta for 5–15 minutes, depending on the size and
type of pasta you are cooking (please see the packet for re-

commended times). The water should cover the pasta at all times. Stir the cooking pasta gently from time to time to prevent sticking. Alternatively, some people add a little oil to the water to prevent sticking. Test the pasta by chewing a piece. It should be easy to bite, but not soggy or doughy. Drain immediately and serve hot with a sauce. To serve cold, drain and immediately rinse under cold water.

Cornucopia Melon

Serves 4

Value Per Portion: Calories: 265.4
Total Fat: 7.9 gm   Fibre: 2.5 gm

2 satsumas *or* mandarins
50 g (2 oz) raisins *or* sultanas
50 g (2 oz) hazelnuts *or* slivered almonds
140 ml (5 fl. oz) orange juice
1 whole honeydew melon

Divide the satsumas into segments and place them in a bowl with the raisins, hazelnuts and orange juice. Stir well and leave to soak for 5–10 minutes. Cut the melon into four and scoop out the seeds. Spoon the fruit mixture on to the melon quarters. Serve immediately.

Country Cabbage Salad

Serves 4

Value Per Portion: Calories: 50.46
Total Fat: .6 gm   Fibre: 1.4 gm

¼ head white cabbage
2 large carrots
1 medium turnip
4 spring onions
50 g (2 oz) fresh watercress
2 stalks celery
5 ml (1 tsp) poppy seed
5 ml (1 tsp) celery seed

Wash, trim and shred the cabbage, carrots and turnip, and place together in a large salad bowl. Trim the spring onions, slice them thinly lengthwise and add to the salad. Wash and trim the watercress and break it into the salad. Wash and thinly slice the celery. Toss all the ingredients together in the bowl and sprinkle the salad with the poppy and celery seeds. Serve with a simple vinaigrette.

Creamy Walnut and Onion Salad

Serves 4
Value Per Portion: Calories: 286.3
Total Fat: 20.5 gm   Fibre: 2.3 gm

1 small turnip
2 large carrots
1 medium onion, peeled
2 eating apples, peeled and cored
115 g (4 oz) broken walnuts
285 g (10 oz) soft tofu
5 ml (1 tsp) caraway seeds
juice of ½ lemon

Wash, trim and shred the turnip and carrots and place them in a salad bowl. Finely chop the onion and apples and add to the salad bowl. Add the remaining ingredients to the salad and stir well. Serve slightly chilled with a garnish of parsley or lemon peel.

Crunchy Pasta Salad

Serves 4
Value Per Portion: Calories: 368.9
Total Fat: 10 gm   Fibre: .5 gm

225 g (8 oz) whole wheat pasta shells
1 × 340 g (12 oz) can sweetcorn
1 large green pepper, seeded
1 large red pepper, seeded
30 ml (2 tbsp) chopped chives *or* 2 spring onions, chopped

Cook the pasta in a pot of boiling water until just tender, about 12 minutes. Drain well and allow to cool. Drain the sweetcorn into a large salad bowl. Wash and thinly slice the peppers and chives (or onions) and place them in the salad bowl. When it is cool, add the pasta and stir all the ingredients together. Serve with a vinaigrette.

Dessert Dates

Serves 4–8
Total Value: Calories: 2180
Total Fat: 84 gm   Fibre: 15 gm

450 g (1 lb) fresh dates
285 g (10 oz) soft tofu
5 ml (1 tsp) ground coriander
115 g (4 oz) walnut halves

Wash the dates, then slice each one in half lengthwise and remove the stone. Do not cut all the way through the dates. Blend the tofu and coriander into a smooth paste and spoon a little into each open date. Press a walnut half on to the filling and place the date on a serving plate. Continue in this way until all the dates are filled. Chill before serving.

Fish Casserole

Serves 4
Value Per Portion: Calories: 181.1
Total Fat: 1.718 gm   Fibre: 0.971 gm

450 g (1 lb) cod, haddock, or plaice, boned and skinned
2 × 225 g (8 oz) cans tomatoes
225 g (8 oz) button mushrooms, washed
15 ml (1 tbsp) finely chopped parsley
freshly ground black pepper

Wash the fish and flake into an ovenproof dish. Empty in the contents of the cans of tomatoes, add the mushrooms and parsley, and season to taste. Bake for about 30 minutes in an oven preheated to 350°F, 180°C, Gas 4.

Fruit and Almond Cake

Serves 6–10
Value for Whole Cake: Calories: 2544
Total Fat: 73 gm   Fibre: 11 gm

450 g (1 lb) whole wheat flour
115 g (4 oz) rolled oats
5 ml (1 tsp) baking powder
2.5 ml (½ tsp) ground ginger
50 g (2 oz) almond flakes
225 g (8 oz) dried currants
50 g (2 oz) citrus peel
30 ml (2 tbsp) oil
570 ml (1 pint) fruit juice

Mix the first five ingredients together in a large mixing bowl. Mix the remaining ingredients together in a jug and leave to one side for 10 minutes. Pre-heat the oven to 350°F, 180°C, Gas 4, and lightly oil a 23 × 33cm (9 × 13 inch) cake tin. Stir the moist ingredients into the dry ingredients. Spoon the batter into the cake tin and bake for 30 minutes. Cool on a wire rack before slicing.

Fruit and Fennel Sauce

Serves 4
Value Per Portion: Calories: 28.75
Total Fat: .2 gm   Fibre: .5 gm

1 large sweet fennel bulb
1 green eating apple, cored
juice of 1 lemon
2.5 ml (½ tsp) ground coriander

Wash and trim the fennel and apple and cut into small chunks. Place in a food processor. Add the lemon juice and the coriander to the processor and purée all the ingredients together to a fine consistency. Serve chilled as a dip for raw vegetables, a garnish in soups or as salad dressing.

Fruit and Nut Muesli

Serves 4
Value Per Portion: Calories: 507.7
Total Fat: 9. gm   Fibre: 6 gm

50 g (2 oz) dried dates
50 g (2 oz) dried figs

1 eating apple, cored
1 banana
50 g (2 oz) raisins
50 g (2 oz) sunflower seeds
285 ml (10 fl. oz) apple juice
50 g (2 oz) rolled oats
2.5 ml (½ tsp) cinnamon

Wash and chop the dates, figs and apple. Peel and slice the banana. Mix all the fruit with the raisins, seeds and apple juice in a large bowl. Add the oats and cinnamon and stir well. Allow to sit for 10 minutes then serve in small bowls.

Fruit Juices

Apple
Serves 1
Value Per 285 ml (10 fl. oz) Calories: 145
Portion:
Total Fat: .35 gm   Fibre: .65 gm

Orange

Serves 1
Value Per 285 ml (10 fl. oz) Calories: 138.8
Portion:
Total Fat: .6 gm   Fibre: .3 gm

Grapefruit

Serves 1
Value Per 285 ml (10 fl. oz) Calories: 120
Portion:
Total Fat: .3 gm   Fibre: .3 gm

Pineapple

Serves 1
Value Per 285 ml (10 fl. oz) Calories: 173.8
Portion:
Total Fat: .25 gm   Fibre: .3 gm

Grape

Serves 1
Value Per 285 ml (10 fl. oz)   Calories: 193.8
Portion:
Total Fat: .2 gm   Fibre: .3 gm

Gardener's Salad

Serves 4
Value Per Portion: Calories: 186.3
Total Fat: 7. gm   Fibre: 1. gm

1 large beetroot
¼ head white cabbage
15 g (½ oz) fresh parsley
4 stalks celery
170 g (6 oz) sweetcorn kernels
115 g (4 oz) dried currants or sultanas
50 g (2 oz) pumpkin or sunflower seeds

Wash, trim and shred the beetroot and cabbage and place them
in a large salad bowl. Wash and finely chop the parsley and add
to the salad. Thinly slice the celery. Add the celery, sweetcorn,
dried fruit and seeds to the salad and stir well. Serve immediately
with a vinaigrette or tofu dressing.

Greek-Style Spinach

Serves 4
Value Per Portion: Calories: 277.4
Total Fat: 7 gm   Fibre: 3.5 gm

170 g (6 oz) dry chickpeas
450 g (1 lb) fresh spinach
15 ml (1 tbsp) olive oil
3 cloves garlic, peeled
2 medium onions, peeled
5 ml (1 tsp) caraway *or* cumin seeds
2.5 ml (½ tsp) freshly ground black pepper

Wash, soak and cook the chickpeas (see page 00). Wash, trim
and drain the spinach. Heat the oil in a deep frying pan or

saucepan over a medium flame. Finely chop the garlic and onion and sauté in the oil, stirring frequently. When the onion is tender, add the caraway and stir well. Add the cooked chickpeas and black pepper, cover the pan and cook for about 5 minutes. Roughly slice the spinach and place on top of the chickpeas. Cover the pan again and leave over a low flame for 10–15 minutes. Do not remove the cover. At the end of this time, stir the spinach into the chickpeas and serve immediately by itself, with rice or with steamed vegetables.

Herbal Teas

Serves 1
Value Per ½ pint (10 fl. oz)   Calories: 1.59
Portion:
Total Fat: .02 gm   Fibre: 0 gm

Herb and Garlic Dressing

Serves 4
Value Per Portion: Calories: 67.67
Total Fat: 7 gm   Fibre: .04 gm

3 cloves garlic, peeled
30 ml (2 tbsp) oil
90 ml (6 tbsp) cider vinegar
10 ml (2 tsp) wet mustard
2.5 ml (½ tsp) dried parsley *or* mixed sweet herbs

Chop or crush the garlic into a jug or jar. Add the other ingredients and shake or stir the mixture very well. Serve over any salad.

Herb and Tomato Salad

Serves 4
Value Per Portion: Calories: 110.9
Total Fat: .5 gm   Fibre: 2 gm

115 g (4 oz) dried butter beans
4 medium tomatoes
2 small onions, peeled

25 g (1 oz) fresh parsley
1 sprig fresh mint

Soak, rinse, drain and pressure cook the beans. Allow them to cool. Coarsely chop the tomatoes and place them in a large salad bowl. Finely chop the onions, parsley and mint and add to the tomatoes. Add the cooled beans and stir well. Chill the salad or serve immediately with a vinaigrette dressing.

Hot Fruit Soup

Serves 4
Value Per Portion: Calories: 152.7
Total Fat: .4 gm   Fibre: .9 gm

2 grapefruit
2 oranges
1 lemon
1 tart apple
50 g (2 oz) raisins

Sauce
140 ml (5 fl. oz) red wine
1.25 ml (¼ tsp) ground cloves
1.25 ml (¼ tsp) ground cinnamon

Carefully peel and section the citrus fruits and place in a shallow casserole dish. Chop the apple and add the apple and raisins to the citrus fruits. Stir well. Prepare the sauce by mixing the wine and spices together in a jug. Pour this over the fruit and allow it to soak for 10 minutes. Stir again. Warm the oven to 325°F, 170°C, Gas 3. Cover the compote and bake for 20 minutes. Serve immediately, pouring a little of the hot sauce over each serving.

Hot Mustard and Chilli Dressing

Serves 4
Value Per Portion: Calories: 80.75
Total Fat: 7 gm   Fibre: .3 gm

1 small fresh chilli
140 ml (5 fl. oz) cider vinegar

juice of 1 lemon
30 ml (2 tbsp) olive oil
5 ml (1 tsp) dry mustard
30 ml (2 tbsp) soya milk

Chop the chilli, including its seeds, very finely and place in a jug or jam jar. Add the remaining ingredients to the jar and stir or shake very well. Serve immediately over salad, baked potato or pasta.

Hot Scandinavian Salad

Serves 4
Value Per Portion: Calories: 245.7
Total Fat: 3.7 gm   Fibre: 1 gm

900 g (2 lb) new potatoes
¼ head white cabbage
3 cloves garlic, peeled
50 g (2 oz) fresh parsley
140 ml (5 fl. oz) cider vinegar
5 ml (1 tsp) dry mustard
15 ml (1 tbsp) olive oil

Scrub the potatoes and steam them until tender. Finely chop the cabbage and garlic and place in a large serving bowl. Wash and chop the parsley. Mix the remaining ingredients together in a small saucepan and bring to a very gentle simmer. When the potatoes are tender, stir them gently into the cabbage and garlic. Now pour the hot vinaigrette over the salad and stir again. Serve immediately.

Hot Tempeh Take-Away

Serves 4
Value Per Portion: Calories: 269.9
Total Fat: 8.5 gm   Fibre: .7 gm

225 g (8 oz) tempeh
10 ml (2 tsp) oil
8 slices whole wheat bread
15 ml (1 tbsp) mild mustard
115 g (4 oz) Cos lettuce leaves

2 medium tomatoes, sliced
½ cucumber, sliced
juice of ½ lemon

Defrost the tempeh and slice the block diagonally in half. Slice each half into four thin wedges and arrange these on a lightly oiled baking tray. Place the tempeh in the oven – at 350°F, 180°C, Gas 4 – for 30 minutes, turning the tempeh wedges after 15 minutes. Or, for a quicker meal, place the tempeh under a hot grill for 10 minutes, turning it after 5 minutes. Meanwhile, lay out the bread, spread four pieces with mustard and arrange the salad ingredients over these four slices. When the tempeh is golden brown, place two wedges on each sandwich, close with the other piece of bread and serve.

Lemon and Peanut Sauce

Serves 4
Value Per Portion: Calories: 29.75
Total Fat: 2 gm   Fibre: .1 gm

15 ml (1 tbsp) unsalted crunchy peanut butter
2 cloves garlic, peeled
juice of 1 lemon
285 ml (10 fl. oz) water

Measure the peanut butter into a small saucepan and place over a medium heat. Finely chop the garlic and add to the peanut butter. Stir often. When the peanut butter is melted, add the lemon juice. Stir well and gradually add the water, stirring after each addition. Reduce the heat and keep covered for 5–10 minutes. Serve hot with rice or vegetables.

Lemon Bean Salad

Serves 4
Value Per Portion: Calories: 40.75
Total Fat: .2 gm   Fibre: .4 gm

115 g (4 oz) dried black-eyed beans
1 bunch fresh coriander leaves
1 large sweet onion, peeled
juice of 1 lemon

2.5 ml (½ tsp) freshly ground black pepper
50 g (2 oz) pimento

Soak the beans and the coriander separately in very cold water overnight. Rinse, drain and pressure-cook the beans. Allow them to cool. Slice the onion very thinly, break each slice into rings and place in a large salad bowl. Pour the lemon juice over the onions and sprinkle with black pepper. Drain, wash and finely chop the coriander.

Add the pimento, coriander and beans to the onions and stir together. Serve immediately or chill for later use.

Lentil Soup

Serves 4
Value Per Portion: Calories: 70.26
Total Fat: .3 gm   Fibre: 2 gm

225 g (8 oz) dried red lentils
1–1.5 litres (2–3 pints) water
1 small green pepper, seeded
1 medium fresh chilli
juice of 1 lemon

Wash the lentils very well, drain them and add them to the fresh water in a large saucepan. Bring to the boil, reduce the heat then cover the pan and simmer for 10 minutes. Wash and chop the pepper and the chilli and add to the lentils. Stir well and cook for a further 20–30 minutes or until the lentils have completely lost their shape and are quite mushy. Stir in the lemon juice just before serving.

Light Vanilla Oat Cake

Serves 4–8
Value of Whole Cake: Calories: 876
Total Fat: 21 gm   Fibre: 4.7 gm

225 g (8 oz) whole wheat flour
50 g (2 oz) rolled oats
50 g (2 oz) raisins *or* sultanas
5 ml (1 tsp) baking powder
2.5 ml (½ tsp) ground cinnamon *or* allspice

15 ml (1 tbsp) oil
5 ml (1 tsp) natural vanilla essence
140 ml (5 fl. oz) water

Warm the oven to 300°F, 160°C, Gas 3, and lightly oil a 20 cm
(8 inch) cake tin. Mix the first five ingredients together in a
mixing bowl. Mix the oil, essence and water, add to the dry
mix and stir well. Spoon the batter evenly into the cake tin and
bake for 25 minutes. Allow to cool, then slice and serve.

Lunch-Box Marinade

Serves 4
Value Per Portion: Calories: 216.4
Total Fat: 1.5 gm   Fibre: 4. gm

The marinade
285 ml (10 fl. oz) cider vinegar
juice of 2 lemons
12 whole cloves
12 whole peppercorns
12 cloves garlic, peeled (optional)
5 ml (1 tsp) caraway seed
140 ml (5 fl. oz) apple juice
3 bay leaves
2 small pieces cinnamon
285–450 ml (10–15 fl. oz) water

The vegetables
225 g (8 oz) carrots
340 g (12 oz) green beans
1 small red pepper, seeded
1 small green pepper, seeded
2 small onions, peeled
1 medium cauliflower
450 g (1 lb) broccoli

Gently heat all the marinade ingredients together in a large
enamel saucepan while you wash and prepare the vegetables.
Thinly slice the carrots, beans, peppers and onions. Cut the
cauliflower and broccoli into florets. Simmer all the vegetables
in the marinade for 15 minutes. Keep the pan covered but stir
occasionally. Remove the pan from the heat, stir the ingredients

well, cover the pan and allow the mixture to cool. Serve immediately or chill and eat over the next 3–4 days.

Monkfish Kebabs

Serves 4
Value Per Portion: Calories: 106
Total Fat: 2.05 gm   Fibre: 0.3 gm

450 g (1lb) monkfish, cut into 4cm (2½ inch) cubes
2 lemons
1 small sprig fresh rosemary, needles removed and finely
  chopped
1 garlic clove, peeled and chopped
freshly ground black pepper
1 green pepper, cored, seeded and cut into small cubes as
above

Sprinkle the monkfish cubes with the juice of 1 lemon. Stir in the rosemary, garlic and seasoning to taste. Cover and leave to marinate for 1 hour. Thread the cubes of fish on to four skewers, alternating with the pepper cubes and small chunks of the remaining lemon. Grill – or barbecue – for about 10 minutes, or until tender, turning often.

Milky Carob Drink

Serves 1
Value Per Portion: Calories: 160.6
Total Fat: 9.9 gm   Fibre: .06 gm

200 ml (7 fl. oz) soya milk
15 ml (1 tbsp) powdered carob

Make as you would hot chocolate. Pour most of the milk into a small saucepan and place over a low heat. Stir the carob into the remaining milk until smooth. Pour the carob mixture into the warm milk and, using a wire whisk, stir to a froth until the milk is hot. Pour immediately into a mug and serve.

Mint and Citrus Drink

Serves 3
Value Per Portion: Calories: 109.9
Total Fat: .2 gm   Fibre: .08 gm

2 grapefruits
2 large oranges
2 lemons
1 lime
1 sprig fresh mint
570 ml (1 pint) sparkling mineral water

Squeeze the fruits and pour their juices together into a large serving jug. Coarsely chop the mint and add to the juice, then pour the mineral water slowly over the juice. Stir gently, chill and serve.

Minty Fruit Salad

Serves 4
Value Per Portion: Calories: 187.3
Total Fat: 1 gm   Fibre: 1.4 gm

1 large grapefruit
2 large oranges
2 eating apples, cored
2 ripe bananas
225 g (8 oz) seedless grapes
1 sprig fresh mint

Peel the grapefruit and oranges and divide them into segments. Cut the segments roughly in half and place in a large serving bowl. Wash and finely chop the apples and add to the citrus. Peel the bananas, slice them into thin rounds and stir them into the fruit salad. Wash the grapes, pull them from their stalks and add to the salad. Stir the whole very well. Chop the mint coarsely and sprinkle over the fruit salad. Serve immediately or chill for an hour before serving.

New Mexico Chilli

Serves 4
Value Per Portion: Calories: 194.3
Total Fat: .8 gm   Fibre: 4.9 gm

570 ml (1 pint) water
1 medium onion, peeled
50 g (2 oz) soya mince
140 g (5 oz) tomato purée
1 × 400 g (14 oz) can chopped tomatoes
1.25–2.5 ml (¼–½ tsp) chilli powder
1 × 450 g (16 oz) can kidney beans, drained
30 ml (2 tbsp) cider vinegar

Measure the water and tip a small amount into a deep saucepan.
Place over a high flame and, when simmering, add the finely
chopped onion. 'Sauté' the onion for 3–5 minutes or until
tender. Add the soya mince, tomato purée, chopped tomatoes
and juices, and the rest of the water and stir well. Reduce the
heat and add the chilli powder and the beans, then cover the
pan and leave to simmer for 25–30 minutes. About 5 minutes
before serving, add the vinegar and stir once again. Serve hot
in bowls.

Nine-to-Five Stew

Serves 4
Value Per Portion: Calories: 614
Total Fat: 2 gm   Fibre: 8.6 gm

450 g (1 lb) swedes
450 g (1 lb) carrots
450 g (1 lb) parsnips
450 g (1 lb) turnips
900 g (2 lb) potatoes
450 g (1 lb) small onions
10 ml (2 tsp) whole cloves
12 peppercorns
450 g (1 lb) unsweetened chestnut purée
2 litres (approx. 4 pints) water

Wash and trim or peel the root vegetables and chop them into

2.5cm (1 inch) pieces. Peel the onions and push a whole clove into both ends of each. Place all the vegetables and the peppercorns into a large stewpot. Mix the chestnut purée with the water in a jug and, when well mixed, pour over the vegetables. Stir the ingredients well. Cover the pot tightly and place it in the oven at a very low heat – 275°F, 140°C, Gas 1 is a perfect setting. If you have an Aga, use the slow oven. Let the stew cook undisturbed for 6–8 hours while you are out at work. Serve hot with fresh bread.

Nut Milk

Serves 2
Value Per Portion: Calories: 332
Total Fat: 29 gm   Fibre: 1.3 gm

115 g (4 oz) cashew nuts and sesame seed mixed, *or* almonds,
   cashew nuts and sesame seed mixed
1.1 litres (2 pints) very cold water
molasses or dried fruit to taste (optional)

Wash the nuts by rinsing them in cool water and draining well. Cover them with the clean water and leave to sit for at least 2 hours or overnight. (Alternatively, if a quick, hot milk is desired, boil the water and soak the nuts in it for 5–10 minutes.) Pour the water and the nuts into a food processor or blender and purée to a very fine consistency. Strain the milk through a piece of cheesecloth and serve immediately. Stir a little molasses into each serving if desired, or add a piece of dried fruit to each glass and pour the milk over.

Onion and Okra Stir-fry

Serves 4
Value Per Portion: Calories: 89.52
Total Fat: 3.8 gm   Fibre: 1.5 gm

450 g (1 lb) fresh okra (ladies' fingers)
3 cloves garlic, peeled
2 small onions, peeled
15 ml (1 tbsp) olive oil
225 g (8 oz) button mushrooms
140–200 ml (5–7 fl. oz) water

Wash the ladies' fingers and cut off the hard tip of each one. Finely chop the garlic and onion and sauté in the olive oil over a high heat. When they are tender, add the ladies' fingers and stir frequently. Clean the mushrooms and add them to the stir-fry. Stir constantly and cook for another 3–4 minutes. Add the water, cover the pan, reduce the heat and cook for 10 minutes longer. Serve immediately with rice, pasta or steamed vegetables.

Onion and Olive Dip

Serves 4
Value Per Portion: Calories: 79.39
Total Fat: 3.4 gm   Fibre: .5 gm

285 g (10 oz) soft tofu
50 g (2 oz) green olives, stoned
2 spring onions
1 eating apple, cored
10 ml (2 tsp) dill or caraway seed

Mash the tofu in a serving bowl. Finely chop the olives and onions and stir into the tofu. Peel and grate the apple into the mixture. Add the dill seed and stir the mixture very well. Chill for 30 minutes before serving.

Orange and Sweet Potato Bake

Serves 4
Value Per Portion: Calories: 132.9
Total Fat: .15 gm   Fibre: 1 gm

450 g (1 lb) sweet potatoes
1 large orange
2.5 ml (½ tsp) freshly ground black pepper

Scrub the sweet potatoes and cut into quarters, cutting only three-quarters of the way through so that you are able to open them. Lay each potato on a piece of foil or arrange them together in a large baking tray. Peel the orange, divide it into segments and cut each segment in half. Place orange pieces in the centre of each 'open' potato and pour any juice in as well. Sprinkle a little black pepper over each potato. Wrap or cover the potatoes and bake at 350°F, 180°C, Gas 4 for 45 minutes. Serve immediately with other vegetables.

Parsley Potato Salad

Serves 4
Value Per Portion: Calories: 121.7
Total Fat: .2 gm   Fibre: .9 gm

450 g (1 lb) new potatoes
115 g (4 oz) carrots
1 bunch spring onions
2–4 sprigs fresh parsley

Scrub and steam the potatoes until tender, then allow them to cool. Scrub and shred the carrots. Trim and thinly slice the onions. Wash and chop the parsley then mix all the ingredients together in a large salad bowl. Serve with a simple vinaigrette or tofu dressing.

Peachy Chicken

Serves 4
Value per portion: Calories: 295.3
Total Fat: 6.498 gm   Fibre: 0.56 gm

4 ripe peaches
45 ml (3 tbsp) orange or lemon juice
5 ml (1 tsp) Dijon mustard
5 ml (1 tsp) chopped fresh parsley
freshly ground black pepper
12 thin slices cooked, skinless chicken

Skin three of the peaches by making a small cut at one end, then plunging them in boiling water for half a minute. Slide off the skins, remove the stones and chop the flesh. Purée this in the liquidizer with the citrus juice, mustard, parsley and seasoning to taste. Chill for about an hour (but no longer, or it will discolour). Spoon a little of the sauce on to each plate, along with three slices chicken, and slices of the remaining peach.

Pea and Tofu Purée

Serves 4
Value Per Portion: Calories: 161.8
Total Fat: 3.3 gm   Fibre: 2.9 gm

450 g (1 lb) cooked peas
285 g (10 oz) soft tofu
1 small onion, peeled
2 cloves garlic, peeled
1 medium tomato
5 ml (1 tsp) paprika

Purée the peas and tofu together in a blender or food processor.
Finely chop the onion, garlic and tomato and add to the blend.
Add the paprika (or chilli powder if you prefer it hot), stir well,
chill and serve with salad and toast.

Plaice with Green Sauce

Serves 4
Value per portion: Calories: 217.9
Total Fat: 4.57 gm   Fibre: 0.64 gm

4 medium plaice fillets, skinned
freshly ground black pepper
finely granted rind of ½ lemon
15 ml (1 tbsp) finely chopped parsley
285 ml (10 fl. oz) skimmed milk
Green sauce
350 g (12 oz) courgettes, trimmed and chopped
285 ml (10 fl. oz) good vegetable stock
finely grated rind of ½ lemon
1 garlic clove, peeled and chopped

Spread the plaice fillets out, skin downwards. Sprinkle with
seasoning to taste, lemon rind and parsley, then roll up. Make
the sauce by cooking the courgettes in the stock with the lemon
rind and garlic until tender, then blend all together until smooth.
Put the plaice 'rolls' into a shallow pan and poach in the milk
with seasoning to taste, until tender, about 8–10 minutes. Drain,
reserving the liquid. Put the 'rolls' in a warm dish, heat the

sauce with a little of the fish poaching liquid, and pour round the 'rolls'. Serve immediately.

Poached Chicken Breast with Vegetables

Serves 4
Value per portion: Calories: 97.42
Total Fat: 2.517 gm   Fibre: 1.313 gm

4 small chicken breasts, boned and skinned
450 ml (15 fl. oz) vegetable stock
freshly ground black pepper
115 g (4 oz) carrots, scrubbed and trimmed
115 g (4 oz) courgettes, trimmed
115 g (4 oz) red pepper, cored and seeded
115 g (4 oz) radishes, trimmed
snipped chives
Sauce
30 ml (2 tbsp) tarragon vinegar
10 ml (2 tsp) Dijon mustard

Poach the chicken breasts in the stock with seasoning to taste for about 20 minutes. Remove from the stock and leave to cool. Reduce the stock by boiling until about 100 ml (4 fl oz) is left. Meanwhile coarsely grate all the vegetables, and mix together. When the reduced stock is cool, mix in the vinegar and mustard to make the sauce. Arrange the cold chicken on plates, surround with the mixed vegetables in mounds (the vegetables could be kept separate if liked), and moisten the mounds with a little of the sauce. Sprinkle with snipped chives.

Saucy Pasta Dish

Serves 4
Value Per Portion: Calories: 464.6
Total Fat: 17 gm   Fibre: .8 gm

225 g (8 oz) whole wheat pasta
15 ml (1 tbsp) oil
1 medium onion, peeled
a pinch of whole wheat flour
285 ml (10 fl. oz) soya milk

2 stalks celery
1 large carrot
285 g (10 oz) sweetcorn
15 g (½ oz) fresh mint

Cook the pasta in a pot of boiling water until just tender, about 12 minutes. In a separate pan, heat the oil and sauté the finely chopped onion until it is tender. Sprinkle a little flour over the sauté and stir well to make a roux. Then gradually add the soya milk, stirring constantly, to make a sauce. Wash and thinly slice the celery; grate the carrot. Add the celery, carrot and sweetcorn to the sauce and stir well. Chop the mint into the sauce and remove from the heat. Drain the pasta and tip it into a large serving bowl. Pour the sauce over, stir well and serve immediately.

Sharp Tomato Sauce

Serves 4
Value Per Portion: Calories: 152.2
Total Fat: .4 gm   Fibre: 1.5 gm

140 ml (5 fl. oz) water
140 ml (5 fl. oz) cider vinegar
4 large prunes
1 lemon
140 g (5 oz) tomato purée
2.5 ml (½ tsp) ground coriander
5 ml (1 tsp) paprika
5 ml (1 tsp) freshly ground black pepper

Mix the water, vinegar and prunes together and leave to one side. Chop the lemon into small pieces and remove the pips. Empty the tomato purée into a small saucepan. Add the lemon pieces and spices and stir well, then add the liquid with the softened prunes. Simmer the mixture over a low heat for 20 minutes, keeping it covered except for one or two stirs. Then remove from the heat, discard the prune stones, and leave the fruit in the sauce. You may leave the lemon pieces in too if you like, as they are attractive. Serve this sauce hot over pasta, rice, vegetables or as the sauce for baked beans.

Simple Almond Milk

Serves 2
Value Per Portion: Calories: 332
Total Fat: 29.8 gm   Fibre: 1.3 gm

115 g (4 oz) whole shelled almonds
1.1 litres (2 pints) very cold water

Measure the almonds into a mixing bowl and cover them with
tepid water. Leave them to soak overnight, or for 8–12 hours.
Drain and rinse the soaked almonds and remove their skins.
This is made easier if you pour a little boiling water over the
soaked almonds. Put the peeled almonds in a food processor
with the cold water. Purée to a very fine, very smooth consistency. Strain the milk through cheesecloth or a paper coffee filter
into a jug. Allow 10–15 minutes for the milk to finish filtering.
Serve this pure white milk immediately. Use the almond pulp in
baking if you wish.

Simple Dhal

Serves 4
Value Per Portion: Calories: 104.4
Total Fat: 3.9 gm   Fibre: 2 gm

225 g (8 oz) red lentils
710 ml (1¼ pints) water
15 ml (1 tbsp) oil
3 cloves garlic, peeled
5 ml (1 tsp) cumin seed, crushed
2 small onions, peeled
2.5 ml (½ tsp) chilli powder
1 small green pepper, seeded

Wash the lentils very well. Place them in a large saucepan, add
the fresh water and bring to a boil over a high heat. Stir the
lentils, cover the pan, reduce the heat and simmer gently. Heat
the oil in a small pan and sauté the finely chopped garlic and
crushed cumin seeds in it, stirring constantly. Finely chop the
onion and add to the sauté. When the onion is tender, add the
chilli powder and chopped pepper. Stir well and remove the
sauté from the heat. When the lentils have simmered for 20

minutes, stir the sauté mixture into them and leave to simmer, covered, for another 5–10 minutes. Serve alone or over rice as a main meal.

Simple September Salad

Serves 4
Value Per Portion: Calories: 105
Total Fat: .3 gm   Fibre: 2.7 gm

680 g (1½ lb) green beans
1 large sweet onion, peeled
4 small new carrots, trimmed
2 eating apples, cored

Wash, trim and steam the green beans (15–20 minutes), and allow them to cool. Thinly slice the onion, break each slice into rings and place in a large salad bowl. Grate the carrots and apples into the salad bowl. Stir well and serve immediately.

Slightly Sweet Tomato Sauce

Serves 4
Value Per Portion: Calories: 71.3
Total Fat: .3 gm   Fibre: 1.1 gm

570 ml (1 pint) water
285 ml (10 fl. oz) cider vinegar
285 g (10 oz) tomato purée
2.5 ml (½ tsp) chilli powder
2.5 ml (½ tsp) ground cloves
3 cloves garlic, peeled
2 small onions, peeled
1 eating apple, cored

Stir the first five ingredients together in a saucepan and place over a medium heat. Bring to a simmer, then reduce the heat. Finely chop the garlic, onion and apple and add to the tomato sauce. Stir well and leave to simmer gently for 20 minutes. Cover and leave off the heat until ready to use. The flavour of this sauce improves if allowed to cool.

Smooth Lentil Pâté

Serves 4
Value Per Portion: Calories: 95.54
Total Fat: .7 gm   Fibre: 1.8 gm

225 g (8 oz) dried red lentils
570–710 ml (1–1¼ pints) water
50 g (2 oz) porridge oats
50 g (2 oz) rice flakes
5 ml (1 tsp) ground black pepper *or* paprika
2.5 ml (½ tsp) ground ginger
25 g (1 oz) fresh coriander leaves

Wash and drain the lentils, add the clean water and bring to a soft boil over a medium heat. Reduce the heat, cover and simmer for 30 minutes, stirring often. Add oats, rice flakes, pepper and ginger and cook for another 5–10 minutes. Wash and chop the coriander. Remove the pâté from the heat, stir in the coriander and spoon into a serving dish. Allow the pâté to cool, then chill or serve immediately.

Sole en Papillote

Serves 4
Value per portion: Calories: 147.6
Total Fat: 1.817 gm   Fibre: 0.373 gm

450 g (1 lb) sole, skinned and boned
50 g (2 oz) celery, trimmed and finely chopped
50 g (2 oz) onions, peeled and finely chopped
50 g (2 oz) carrots, scrubbed and finely chopped
50 g (2 oz) fennel, trimmed and finely chopped
fresh chopped fresh herbs (dill or fennel)
15 ml (1 tbsp) lemon juice
5 ml (1 tsp) finely grated lemon rind
finely ground black pepper

Divide the fish into four even portions, and blanch the finely chopped vegetables in boiling water for about 2 minutes. Cut four 20cm (8 inch) squares of good greaseproof paper and divide the drained blanched vegetables between them, mounding them in the centre. Place a piece of fish on top of each mound of vegetables, and season with herbs, lemon juice and rind, and pepper to taste. Bring the paper together to form a triangle, and fold over the edges to seal completely. Put the package on a baking tray and cook in an oven preheated to 400°F, 200°C, Gas 6 for 8–10 minutes. Serve immediately.

Spanish-Style Rice and Vegetables

Serves 4
Value Per Portion: Calories: 332.2
Total Fat: 1.8 gm   Fibre: 2.1 gm

225 g (8 oz) whole grain rice
850 ml (1½ pints) water
5 ml (1 tsp) turmeric
1 bay leaf
1 × 5cm (2 inch) piece cinnamon
2 small onions, peeled
1 small red pepper, seeded
1 small green pepper, seeded
285 g (10 oz) fresh *or* frozen peas

Wash and drain the rice. Bring the water to a low boil and add the turmeric, bay leaf and cinnamon stick. Stir well, then add the rice and bring to the boil again. Cover and simmer for 10 minutes. Finely chop the onions and peppers. Stir the onions, peppers and peas into the cooking rice and cover the pan once more. Cover the pan and cook until the liquid is absorbed. Serve hot or cold.

Special Spuds

Serves 4
Value Per Portion: Calories: 281.8
Total Fat: 2.8 gm   Fibre: 1.5 gm

4 large potatoes
285 g (10 oz) soft tofu
1 small onion, peeled
1 medium tomato
5 ml (1 tsp) dried parsley
10 ml (2 tsp) brewer's yeast

Scrub the potatoes, pierce them and bake in a hot oven – at about 425°F, 220°C, Gas 7 – for 45 minutes, or until well cooked. Mash the tofu in a mixing bowl. Finely chop the onion and tomato and add to the tofu. Add the parsley and yeast and stir the mixture very well. Cut the potatoes in half and spoon one-quarter of the tofu whip over each potato. Sprinkle with a little pepper if desired. Serve hot alone or with a salad.

Spicy Banana Milkshake

Serves 4
Value Per Portion:
Total Fat: 8.6 gm

Calories: 250.2
Fibre: .8 gm

2–3 ripe bananas
570 ml (1 pint) soya milk
2.5 ml (½ tsp) ground allspice

Peel the bananas and break them into a large blender. Add the milk and allspice and whisk to a thick, even consistency. Serve immediately or chill for 10 minutes. Garnish with a sprig of rosemary or cinnamon stick.

Spicy Carrot Sauté

Serves 4
Value Per Portion:
Total Fat: .6 gm

Calories: 87.93
Fibre: 2.2 gm

3 cloves garlic
60 ml (2 fl. oz) apple juice
30 g (1 oz) fresh ginger, peeled
450 g (1 lb) carrots, scrubbed
1 bunch spring onions

Peel and chop the garlic and 'sauté' in the apple juice over a high heat. Thinly slice the ginger and trimmed carrots and add to the sauté, stirring frequently. Wash and trim the onions, slice them lengthwise and add to the sauté. However, do not stir them in yet – leave them on top of the carrots. Cover the pan and reduce the heat. Leave covered for 10 minutes then remove the cover, stir the vegetables well, and serve with rice.

Spicy Raisin Cake

Serves 6–10
Value for Whole Cake: Calories: 1626
Total Fat: 70.9 gm   Fibre: 19.5 gm

115 g (4 oz) whole wheat flour
115 g (4 oz) rolled oats
50 g (2 oz) oat bran
115 g (4 oz) raisins *or* sultanas
2.5 ml (½ tsp) ground cinnamon
2.5 ml (½ tsp) ground cloves
5 ml (1 tsp) baking powder
285 ml (10 fl. oz) water *or* fruit juice
30 ml (2 tbsp) oil

Pre-heat the oven to 350°F, 180°C, Gas 4, and lightly oil a 20cm (8 inch) baking tin. Mix the dry ingredients together in a large mixing bowl. Measure the water or fruit juice and oil together into a jug and pour gradually into the dry mix, stirring well after each addition. Spread the batter evenly into the cake tin and bake for 30 minutes. Cool slightly before removing it from the tin. Cool on a wire rack.

Spinach and Chicken Parcels

Serves 4
Value per portion: Calories: 139.4
Total Fat: 3.73 gm   Fibre: 0.156 gm

285 g (10 oz) chicken breast, boned and skinned
1 egg white
lemon juice
freshly ground black pepper
5 ml (1 tsp) olive oil
25 g (1 oz) brown rice
60 ml (2 fl. oz) vegetable stock
20 undamaged spinach or cabbage leaves, thick stalks removed

Place the chicken, cut into pieces, with the egg white and 1 teaspoon lemon juice into the food processor, and blend until smooth. Add some seasoning to taste, and then chill for about

30 minutes. Meanwhile, heat the oil in a pan, stir in the rice, and then add the stock. Simmer, covered, until the water has been absorbed, when the rice will only be part cooked. Cool. Blanch the spinach leaves in boiling water, then drain and dry thoroughly. Mix the cold part-cooked rice into the fish mixture and divide between the spinach leaves. Wrap up to form a parcel, and pack into a greased dish in one layer. Pour over a mixture of 15 ml (1 tbsp) lemon juice and 15 ml (1 tbsp) water, and place the dish in a roasting tin full of hot water. Bake, covered, in an oven preheated to 350°F, 180°C, Gas 4 for about 1 hour. Serve hot or cold.

Split Pea Soup

Serves 4
Value Per Portion: Calories: 176.3
Total Fat: .6 gm   Fibre: 1.9 gm

225 g (8 oz) dried split green peas
1.1 litres (2 pints) water
1 strip kombu (seaweed, see page 63, optional)
1 bunch fresh coriander
6 cloves garlic
freshly ground black pepper to taste

Wash and drain the peas and place them in a deep saucepan. Add the water, cover and bring to the boil. Add the kombu, reduce the heat and simmer for 45 minutes, stirring occasionally. Wash and pick over the coriander and chop it finely. Peel the garlic and cut each clove in half. Add the coriander, garlic and pepper to the soup. Stir well and simmer for a further 15 minutes. Serve very hot.

Stuffed Pumpkin Bake

Serves 4
Value Per Portion: Calories: 80.7
Total Fat: 1. gm   Fibre: 2.5 gm

1 × 900 g (2 lb) squash or pumpkin
340 g (12 oz) broccoli
25 g (1 oz) fresh parsley

3 cloves garlic, peeled
1 medium onion, peeled

Slice the squash in half lengthwise and remove the seeds. Place each half on a large piece of aluminium foil. Chop the remaining ingredients very finely and blend them together in a mixing bowl. You may add a dash of black pepper if you like. Divide this filling between the two halves of squash and press well down – even so the filling will rise above the edges of the squash. Bring the edges of the aluminium foil up over the filling and fold them together in a seal. Place the filled squash halves together on a roasting tray and bake at 350°F, 180°C, Gas 4 for 30–40 minutes. Serve hot with a favourite sauce.

Sunday-Best Mixed Grill

Serves 1
Value Per Portion: Calories: 445.1
Total Fat: 12.6 gm   Fibre: 9.8 gm

1 vegetarian burger (that can be grilled)
2 medium tomatoes, halved
50 g (2 oz) mushrooms
2 slices whole wheat bread
85 g (3 oz) sugarless baked beans
30 ml (2 tbsp) tomato ketchup *or* brown sauce

Place the burger under a hot grill with the tomatoes and mushrooms. Toast the bread and heat the baked beans. Pour the beans over one piece of toast if you like, add the sauce and serve.

Sweet and Sour Spaghetti Sauce

Serves 4
Value Per Portion: Calories: 254.8
Total Fat: 1 gm   Fibre: .6 gm

1 medium onion, peeled
3 cloves garlic, peeled
60 ml (2 fl. oz) cider vinegar
225 g (8 oz) button mushrooms
50 g (2 oz) raisins *or* currants

15 ml (1 tbsp) brewers' yeast
5 ml (1 tsp) freshly ground black pepper
115 g (4 oz) whole wheat spaghetti

Chop onion and garlic and 'sauté' in the vinegar in a large frying pan. Clean and thickly slice the mushrooms and add to the sauté. Stir in the raisins, yeast and pepper, stir well and simmer very gently while you cook the spaghetti. Serve the sauce over the spaghetti.

Tangy Tempeh Marinade

Serves 4
Value Per Portion: Calories: 127.6
Total Fat: 4.4 gm   Fibre: .3 gm

225 g (8 oz) tempeh
140 ml (5 fl. oz) cider vinegar
juice of 2 lemons
5 ml (1 tsp) mustard seed
12 whole cloves
12 whole peppercorns
3–6 cloves garlic, peeled (optional)
2 small onions, peeled
1 tart apple, cored

Defrost the tempeh and cut into 2.5cm (1 inch) cubes. Place the tempeh in a casserole dish. Mix the vinegar, lemon juice, seeds and spices together in a jug. Finely chop the garlic, onions and apple and add to the marinade in the jug. Stir well and pour over the tempeh pieces in the casserole. Cover the casserole and leave the tempeh to marinate for 4–8 hours. Bake, covered, at 350°F, 180°C, Gas 4 for 30 minutes. Remove the cover and bake for a further 10 minutes if you want a crispy surface to the tempeh. Serve hot with brown rice and steamed broccoli.

Tea-Time Toast and Jam

Serves 1
Value Per Portion: Calories: 189.4
Total Fat: 9.2 gm   Fibre: .4 gm

2 thick slices whole wheat bread

30 ml (2 tbsp) sugarless jam
30 ml (2 tbsp) Granose or Vitaquel

Toast the bread and spread with jam and margarine.

Note: the analysis is given for the jam and the margarine. If you would rather, have one or the other on your toast to reduce the calories and/or fat content.

Thick Broccoli Soup

Serves 4
Value Per Portion: Calories: 223.7
Total Fat: 12 gm   Fibre: 2.6 gm

15 ml (1 tbsp) oil
1 small onion, peeled
3 cloves garlic, peeled (optional)
10 ml (2 tsp) whole wheat flour
570 ml (1 pint) soya milk
1.1 litres (2 pints) water
900 g (2 lb) broccoli
5 ml (1 tsp) freshly ground black pepper

Heat the oil in a deep enamel saucepan. Finely chop the onion and garlic and sauté over a medium heat for 3 minutes. Sprinkle the flour over the sauté and stir well to make a roux. Mix the soya milk with the water and gradually add to the roux, stirring well after each addition. When all the liquid has been added, reduce the heat and cover the pan. Wash and coarsely chop the broccoli and add to the soup. Add the black pepper and allow the soup to simmer gently for 15–20 minutes, stirring occasionally. You may leave the broccoli in chunks, mash them slightly as you stir, or run the soup through a mouli for an even texture. Serve hot.

Tomato and Tofu Soup

Serves 4
Value Per Portion: Calories: 53.19
Total Fat: 1.4 gm   Fibre: .6 gm

4 small courgettes
115 g (4 oz) firm tofu

1 medium onion, peeled
1.1 litres (2 pints) water
140 g (5 oz) tomato purée
2.5 ml (½ tsp) freshly ground black pepper
5 ml (1 tsp) dried basil

Wash and trim the courgettes, then slice into thin rounds. Drain the tofu and cut into small cubes. Thinly slice the onion. Mix the water and tomato purée together in a jug then stir in the black pepper and basil. Place a large saucepan over a medium flame and heat it for 2–3 minutes. Then pour approximately 60 ml (2 fl. oz) of the tomato sauce into the pan so that it bubbles immediately. Drop the onion into the sauce and stir constantly as you would a sauté. Add more sauce if necessary. When the onions have softened, add the courgettes and continue to stir over a medium to high heat for 3 minutes. Add the remaining sauce, stir well and cover the pan. Reduce the heat and leave it to simmer gently for 15 minutes. Add the tofu, stir the soup and leave it over the heat for a further 5 minutes. Serve hot.

Vegetable Juices

Serving size and nutritional value of vegetable juices will vary greatly according to the quality of vegetables used, the season and, of course, the type of vegetable used. Please see the information in Chapter Five, *The Liquids Only Diet*, for approximate serving sizes derived from a measure of vegetables.

Method:
Scrub the vegetables and trim the tough, woody or inedible portions. A juicer is the most efficient means of extracting the juices from vegetables – please follow manufacturer's instructions. Some juices may be made, but less efficiently, with a blender and food processor. Purée the vegetable, adding a small amount of water if necessary. When it reaches a smooth liquid state, strain through cheesecloth. Chill or serve immediately. Try to drink these juices as soon as possible after making to gain full nutritional benefit.

Whole Wheat Bread

Serves 1
Value Per 2 Slices: Calories: 122
Total Fat: 1.6 gm   Fibre: .4 gm